THE ARISTOTELIAN ANALYSIS OF USURY

ODD LANGHOLM

THE ARISTOTELIAN ANALYSIS OF USURY

UNIVERSITETSFORLAGET AS
BERGEN · OSLO · STAVANGER · TROMSØ

ISBN 82-00-07290-8

Distribution offices:

NORWAY
Universitetsforlaget
P.O. Box 2977, Tøyen
0608 Oslo 6

UNITED KINGDOM
Global Book Resources Ltd.
109 Great Russell Street
London WC1B 3NA

UNITED STATES and CANADA
Columbia University Press
136 South Broadway
Irvington-on-Hudson
New York, NY 10533

Published with a grant from
the Norwegian Research Council
for Science and the Humanities

Printed in Norway by
Reklametrykk A.s, Bergen

Preface

This volume completes a series of studies of different areas and features of medieval Aristotelian economic doctrine. My previous contributions (see Bibliography: Langholm (1)-(3)) circle around the subject of usury without going into it properly and now serve as essential supports for the present analysis. It is now more than twenty-five years since John T. Noonan published his monumental study of scholastic usury doctrine. I do not aim to compete with that admirable scholarly work, which I trust will remain a standard reference for at least as many years to come. Going into legal and procedural history in considerable detail, Noonan's scope is much broader than mine, which is strictly limited to the rational arguments ("the natural law case") against usury. Within that scope, some improvement in our understanding of the scholastics can be achieved by establishing an analogy between usury doctrine and the doctrine of the just price in commodity exchange (Langholm (1) and (2)) and by basing the explanation of usury doctrine on a more correct interpretation of the scholastic theory of money (Langholm (3)).

A small number of recently discovered medieval treatises on usury serve as a basis for this reassessment. Centrally placed in the tradition and highly influential, they call for a focus on the Aristotelian concept of the sterility of money as a crux for the scholastic doctrine, not merely as a colourful classical allusion (in which capacity it has been summarily dismissed by some historians) but as an analytical concept. As such it was developed from Aristotle's simple biological simile into a theoretical proposition which went to the core of the scholastics' vision of the economy whose participants they sought to guide. It was a near-stationary coin economy, without proper money markets, where money had to be borrowed at usury, not necessarily for consumption purposes, but usually to get out of some present predicament rather than in the expectation of creating a real surplus. Under such conditions, usury is robbery, as the scholastics said, because money is barren, and it may well be said to be barren in a certain modern sense of the word: Coins can bear no fruit when they serve only as a medium of exchange in a non-growth economy. Schumpeter's "vision" of the zero interest stationary state is easily detected in the last statement, and I gladly acknowledge my debt to a writer who was not only a great economist but the greatest historian of economics.

Textual research in the early Latin sources of the history of economics requires a multiple expertise unfortunately not easily attained by a single person and seldom found even in a single academic institution. In the course of the years it has taken me to complete this series of studies I have had the good fortune to be able to return from frequent research excursions to the fruitful interdisciplinary milieu of the University and School of Economics in Bergen, and I would like to take this opportunity to thank a number of colleagues, whether linguists, philosophers, historians or economists, who cheerfully guided and corrected my advance through this complex material. For financial support I thank the *Norwegian Research Council for Science and the Humanities* and the *Bank of Norway Foundation for Research in Economics.*

O. L.

Contents

1. Objectives and sources

It is bound to happen sometimes in the political and social sciences that some important new insight which opens up promising future vistas will also enable historians of that science to understand better some past phase in its development, which has remained for a time an unexplained oddity. I believe that the recent theoretical preoccupation with the problems of growth, and more specifically with the complicated role played by money in growth models, may have provided an opportunity of this nature for the historian of economics, and it is in that belief that I propose in the present study to go back once more and try to make sense of the scholastic theory of usury. No single subject fills more pages of medieval economic writing than usury does, and no part of scholastic doctrine has received more attention from historians than the rejection of claims to profit over and above the principal in money loans. But except for the occasional moral or confessional apologist, few historians have found much scientific merit in the philosophical constructions of the scholastics regarding usury. On the contrary, criticism was able to develop to a point where usury doctrine stood for all that was unscientific and irrational in our professional heritage. It had become a symbol of the intellectual sophistry and moral hypocrisy of medieval thought. For someone familiar with scholastic economic sources who has found in them much reasoning adequate to their times and circumstances, their peculiar stand against usury must pose the ultimate analytical challenge.

If the explanation of price is the core of economic science, then the price of money is the core of capitalism. As the Middle Ages drew to a close, the circumvention of the Church's ban on usury, which was to occupy the late Catholic moralists, no less than the open rejection of the ban by some early Protestant teachers, came to symbolize, in the minds of historians, the very spirit of a new age. By the same token, the admission that interest on money is a necessary fact of economic life, fostering a legitimate curiosity and leading to systematic enquiry into its causes and manifestations, marked for posterity the dawn of economic science proper. While sophistry and hypocrisy are to my mind misleading clues to scholastic economics, capitalism is of course a clue to the development of modern economics and therefore, by negation, a clue to something significant in what it replaced. As such it is partly of an ideological nature (the scholastics would say: of an ethical nature), and we cannot object to following it for that reason. But it is not of that nature exclusively.

We are experiencing today an advanced stage (some believe a near final stage) of a social system which the scholastics could see only in embryo. It is often hard for analytical development to keep pace with historical development. Even at the present late stage, which encourages exploration of previously unsuspected extreme areas, new and apparently very significant analytical premises of capitalistic economics are being pointed out. Now it is logically true that carrying an analytical system to one extreme may sometimes reveal the nature of limiting conditions valid at a different extreme. To be more precise, the more reliance we place on growth in order to explain interest (which is characteristic of nearly all post-Wicksellian approaches to dynamic economics), the more relevant may the stationary character of the scholastic vision of society be as a clue to a theory which prohibits usury. That vision, shaping their analysis, was certainly in part ideological, at least in the sense that it was only imperfectly founded on a realistic assessment of the material conditions already prevailing at the time when it was held; but that is true of most analytical models in economics. Yet it may not have been as false as it has been made out to be. Within the safe confines of the self-evident capitalistic system, that is, from the point of view (let us say) of Walrasian statics, usury doctrine is inexplicable. That was the kind of viewpoint subconsciously adopted by most late nineteenth- and early twentieth-century historians of medieval economics. It is still common. In recent years it is within the ranks of economists challenging neo-classical conceptions rather than within the ranks of historians that the suggestion has been voiced that the scholastics may merit a reappraisal.

More often than not, the object of this kind of reappraisal is Aristotle, and so it is to be in the present book. The scholastics must be explained in their own terms, and only rarely did they anticipate the analytical terms used by present-day economists in their approach to similar problems. The most I can promise is to establish, towards the end of this study, some tentative conceptual correlations. In the Middle Ages, and increasingly so from the thirteenth century when this study picks up momentum, the great source of conceptual structures was the scientific system of Aristotle. As a matter of fact, the ancient Greek philosopher made a number of distinct contributions to the foundations of economics, most of them extracted from the Latin version of his works by the medieval scholastics. But if the modern economist associates Aristotle's name with his field of study at all, what will come first to his mind is most likely the strange proposition that money is barren, sterile, and therefore cannot (or rather ought not to) support any interest. This, it is often alleged, the scholastics took from Aristotle's *Politics* and on it they based much of their rational argumentation against usury. It is consequently around the concept of sterility rather than around the concept of stationariness that this study is built; what I propose to show is that they must in the end be analytically related.

Unfortunately, cursory inspection of medieval sources may fail to unearth much of the kind of rational argumentation mentioned above and indeed find much material substance to the scholastics' remarks about sterility. It often seems to reduce to the type of ancient saying with which they were so fond of bolstering preconceived opinions. Scholars therefore disagree about the true foundations of usury doctrine and about Aristotle's role in it. In the opinions of Schaub (long the central authority on the history of usury theory) and of Troeltsch (the unrivalled authority on the history of Christian social science in general), it depended heavily on the concept of the sterility of money.[1] Noonan, the author of a more recent comprehensive study of the doctrine (replacing that of Schaub as the standard text), while admitting its influence, considers the Aristotelian principle of sterility to have had chiefly a popular appeal, and consequently accords it no more than middle rank among the many rational arguments against usury put forward by the scholastics.[2]

Nevertheless, Noonan (though he lacks some of the best sources) provides an important springboard for the present study because he takes these various arguments seriously as representing the positive analytical element in usury doctrine, tracing them through the tradition and subjecting them to logical scrutiny. By contrast, as already indicated, there is no lack of modern insinuations that the usury arguments were driven to desired conclusions by political and ideological convenience, perhaps even by the economic interests of the medieval Church itself. Such differences of opinion raise a number of side issues which must plague a study like the present one but are not its primary objective. I am not much concerned here with the relative importance of Aristotelian elements in the scholastic model, as compared with other sources of support for the ban on usury. Nor do I see it as intrinsically worthwhile to assess how far extraneous interests interfered with the terms and confused the conclusions of scholastic reasoning, though we must bear in mind that they may have done so to a considerable extent.

The scholastics purported to base their theory of usury partly on natural reason, and it is from those sections of some of their long discussions that the material for the present study is derived. Nevertheless, their conclusions were not based on reason alone, but on reason influenced by authority, ideology

[1] Schaub 62n, Troeltsch 346; cf. also Funk (1) 125, (3) 45, Endemann II, 359, Fanfani 15.

[2] Noonan 395.

and convenience. Just as, indeed, those changing theories have been based, by which the scholastic one was replaced. There will always be a point where one's analytical arguments take off from assumptions accepted on the authority of one's teachers, and there will always be aspects of those assumptions and arguments which are coloured by ideology, and aspects of ideology which are coloured by convenience. To cleanse one's reasoning of such impurities (if "impurities" they are) is never fully possible. In the case of research into scholastic economics it may not be out of place to recommend that we look as keenly for preconceptions disturbing our critical outlook as for those allegedly hidden in the material under study.

When this is said, let it be added that scholastic economics was an ethical system. It pretended to be nothing else. Its analytical elements are reasoning from ethical premises. To criticize such a theoretical system is partly to reveal those premises which may be foreign to us and difficult to understand. Chains of reasoning in the system may then be submitted to tests for inconsistency both to see if they are valid and constructive on those premises and to see if they may permit changes and generalizations in the ethical basis. What I shall try to show in this book is that it is possible to extract from the mass of scholastic writing about usury certain slender threads which I believe to be genuinely analytical in character and genuinely Aristotelian in origin, and that they make good sense in their proper historical setting and perhaps even contribute to the kind of fundamental theory which reaches beyond historical accident.

Considerable additions to available source material partly account for these results and for the analytical departures which led to them. Among those additions are some of the recently catalogued medieval commentaries on Aristotle's works, which I have analysed in two previous books.[3] However, in the case of usury "Aristotelian" sources and arguments must be taken in a broader sense, for the sterility idea travelled much farther away

[3] Langholm (1) and (3).

from the original texts and commentaries than did most other Aristotelian concepts. More important among recent discoveries is therefore a small set of proper economic treatises which make use of that idea. They do not cling closely to any particular text or tradition, but the authors all knew Aristotle well (one of them was also a commentator) and developed his suggestions forcefully. Written at a crucial period, exceptionally explicit and influential, these works yet suffered oblivion for a long time and were never examined before for our present purpose (and in some key instances hardly for any other purpose). Two analytical ideas were born of reading them and comparing them with familiar texts. One of these ideas was to conceive of the principle of the sterility of money not as something given once and for all but as a concept in development. The other one was to view this developed concept as an element of a larger system of economic ethics which the scholastics constructed on the basis of Aristotle. Before proceeding to a presentation of these important new sources (introducing them by way of the various scholastic genres which surrounded them), it is useful to make some preliminary observations about each of these analytical ideas.

It is not difficult to understand how a reader of standard scholastic texts can get the impression that the sterility of money is mainly a cliché which meant little analytically. So it undoubtedly was to many early authors who referred to it briefly in its original version. It is not as though it was the only argument employed against usury. It was one among many. Some of the other arguments might also rest on Aristotle. Some had developed from origins in Roman or canon law, or with the Church Fathers. Some were of the scholastics' own making. In cursory discussions of principles, little reliance might be placed on the sterility propositions as read in Aristotle's *Politics*. However, not all the rational arguments against usury fared equally well. Some were openly rejected by the scholastics themselves at an early date; or abandoned in silence; or modified. No two lists of arguments were exactly alike; there were endless variations and permutations. If rejects are discarded and variants reduced, there remains a much shorter list of arguments; four or five parallel lines of reasoning to the conclusion that usury is unnatural. But these parallel arguments are not mutually independent either. I think it can be shown that it is really the sterility principle which is at work in all of them. In a few crucial works a way was found to restate the ancient argument in such a way as to underpin and thus eventually to absorb those among the alternative arguments which were not by then ignored or rejected. Those which survived seemed to retain only a borrowed validity in so far as they could be read as different ways of saying the same thing. Much of this reduction is quite explicit. It is not only that we can now reason out those relationships; the scholastics themselves pointed them out.

It follows from this discovery that some of the most interesting analysis of the principle of sterility is not to be found under that heading at all but under different headings. In fact, the proposition that money is sterile no longer meant either what Aristotle himself probably took it to mean or what some of the earliest commentators seem to have read into it. Separated from its literary roots, it could be revamped to accommodate the requirements of a more advanced theory. This episode is not at all unique in the annals of Aristotelianism. Ancient constructs, reinterpreted, can often be seen to have served as analytical vehicles along lines hardly envisaged by Aristotle, owing to a unique intellectual acumen and an immense authority, as well as to the ubiquity of the Aristotelian texts, which caused everybody to come back to him and think in his terms.

Judged in this way, the concept of the sterility of money certainly played a prominent part in the scholastic reasoning about usury. Nevertheless it is subsidiary to some other Aristotelian principles which (developed in similar ways) shaped the moral and analytical system which made use of the sterility concept. Their significance emerges if one relates the theory of usury (being the price paid for the use of money) to the scholastic theory of pricing in general. With the first modern generation of scholars who turned their attention to medieval economics, this relationship was a simple matter: a peculiar kind of labour theory of value was believed to be at work in both fields. Later the labour interpretation of scholastic just price doctrine came under heavy criticism and was more or less completely abandoned in favour of a demand interpretation, thus severing this simple connection between the main areas of scholastic economics and leaving usury doctrine at a loose end, seemingly more unreasonable than ever before.

If by this study I can hope to achieve anything more than bring to the general attention of scholars some highly interesting new sources on usury (for others to draw their own conclusions from), it would be to demonstrate that there is after all a meaningful and significant relationship between the principles underlying the scholastic theories of justice in the exchange of commodities and in the lending of money. It is not to be found by comparing the merits of a labour theory and a demand theory of value. On the contrary, I believe that comparison to be misleading if applied to scholastic economics, in which cost and market served merely as mutually supporting criteria to estimate reasonable terms of exchange in exceptional cases. The normal case was to leave the bargaining about terms to the parties themselves, as it must be in any market society. Scholastic just price doctrine can then be approached from two points of view: either as a set of criteria for determining whether there is such duress (or similar infringement) as to invalidate the conditions of free bargaining; or as a set of criteria for estimating value equivalence when there is such duress.

The concept of economic duress and the concept of just equivalence were both developed from Aristotle. They are fundamental to all scholastic economic ethics. The model sketched above applies to usury as well, up to the point where the sterility of money makes a difference. To make what I believe to be the most fruitful approach to usury doctrine, I shall give full attention to the scholastic analysis of commodity pricing in the chapter which follows, drawing some preliminary analogies to usury, then devote four chapters to the scholastic natural law arguments against usury and show how they converge on the sterility proposition, before concluding with a chapter which picks up the thread again from Chapter 2 and shows, partly in the light of new theoretical insight, that in a stationary vision of society a positive price for the use of money must always be the result of duress. In this present chapter I must devote the remaining pages to guiding the reader to those texts which are mainly of interest for this kind of doctrinal enquiry.

*

These actually make up only a small part of the total body of medieval literature on usury. In that literature taken as a whole, more space is given to explaining *when* usury occurs than to *why* it is forbidden and more to authority than to rational arguments against it. Standard business practice embraced a number of different types of contract, and many hypothetical variants might be imagined whose usurious character needed to be clarified. As pressure on the doctrine increased, certain arrangements would also be concocted by which it might be deliberately circumvented, giving rise to some questionable casuistry on the part of its defenders. While this aspect is undoubtedly exaggerated in the unsympathetic judgment of posterity, there is no denying most scholastics' hurry to get on with cases, and most of this makes discouraging reading for the scholar searching for general principles. True, principles must be invoked to solve cases, and some recurrent applications are revealing. Nevertheless, in many of the sources examined for the purpose of the present study, the material actually used belongs in brief introductory sections.

Fair coverage of positive doctrine is to be found in some theological works. They include the great *summae*, a number of commentaries on the *Sentences* of Peter Lombard (the patristic compilation on the Bible), *quodlibeta* (chosen questions for dispute), and some other types.[4] However, authors contributing

[4] Theological works and editions quoted: William of Auxerre (d. 1231), *Summa aurea*, Paris 1500; Alexander of Hales (d. 1245), *Summa theologica*, Book III (=Vol.IV), Quaracchi 1948; Bonaventura (d. 1274), *Commentarius in tertium librum Sententiarum* (henceforth: *Sent.*III), in *Opera*, Vol.III, Quaracchi 1887, and *Collationes de decem praeceptis*, in *Opera*, Vol.V, Quaracchi

to these genres were inclined (as might be expected) to rely mostly on scriptural authority rather than argument when explaining why usury was forbidden. They could have a field day firing off the Old Testament battery of denunciations, clinching their cases by citing the single alleged utterance by Christ on the subject (in the Sermon on the Mount, as reported by Luke): "Lend, hoping for nothing again." It is tempting to rely on support of this quality, and most scholastic authors would have some resort to it, even those who drew on other traditions and most forcefully developed the natural law case. Thus Olivi (one of the new discoveries to be presented below), before arguing in seven points that usury is against natural equity, quotes nine places in the Bible to show that it is against divine law, adding for good measure the teachings of five saints and Roman popes. Odonis (another discovery), while quarrelling with Olivi over these arguments, pretends to reject all of them and rest his own case solely on Luke 6.

But no Christian author could seriously reject natural law and put his trust in divine law alone as a basis of social morality, for natural law is a part of divine law. Its importance as a fundament of usury doctrine is stated most succinctly much later on in the scholastic tradition by Francis of Vitoria, the Dominican professor and commentator on Aquinas who founded the famous "School of Salamanca". What Christ says about usury in the Gospel according to Luke, says Vitoria, is a counsel not a precept, and that is all there is about usury in the New Testament. There is a lot in the Old Testament, but Christ has liberated us from the burden of the Old Law, *except in so far as*

1891; Albert the Great (d. 1280), *Sent.*III, in *Opera*, Vol.28, Paris 1894; Thomas Aquinas (d. 1274; works – or parts of those works used here - in chronological order, with volume number in *Opera*, Parma 1852-73), *Sent.*III (7), *Super Lucam* (12), *De malo* (8), *Quodlibeta* (9), *Summa theologiae*,II-II (3), *Postilla super Psalmos* (14); Henry of Ghent (d. 1293), *Quodlibeta*, Paris 1518; Giles of Rome (d. 1316), *Quodlibeta*, Venice 1504; John Duns Scotus (d. 1308), *Sent.*IV, in *Opera*, Vol.18, Paris 1894; Richard of Middleton (d. 1307/8), *Sent.*IV, Brescia 1591; Francis of Meyronnes (d. c. 1328), *Sent.*IV, Venice 1520; Durandus of Saint-Pourçain (d. 1332), *Sent.*III, Venice 1571; and (to represent the later tradition) Gabriel Biel (d. 1495), *Sent.*IV, Lyon 1514.

it follows from natural law. Hence there is no valid Christian precept condemning usury except the precepts of natural law.[5] Now the question as to whether Luke 6 contains a counsel or a precept is a much disputed one, just as the reading of the text itself is in doubt.[6] If no valid case can be made against usury in natural law, and Christ still *forbids* usury, then Christ's teaching is against natural law. To hold that would be heresy. If, on the other hand, Christ only advises us not to charge anything above the principal in the repayment of a loan while there is nothing in *law* against it, then the road is wide open to admitting moderate usury under given circumstances. The only way to block this is by showing that usury *is* against natural law. Scholastic authors might dispute how best to state the case, just as Olivi and Odonis did. That is how their economic theory evolved.

Natural law was a diffuse and changing concept. However, it is clear that it was partly embedded in human law. On the very eve of Aristotle's appearence in the West, the Roman law became generally available again. At more or less the same time, Church legislation (as well as some less official patristic teaching) was codified in the volumes of canon law, first in Gratian's *Decretum*, then in the *Decretals* of Gregory IX (in five books) and finally in Boniface VIII's addition to it, known as the *Sextum*. All these compilations have sections on usury, which drew a truly enormous volume of commentary. Unfortunately,

[5] Vitoria, *Comentarios a la Secunda secundae de Santo Tomás*, Tom.IV, *De iustitia*, in *Biblioteca de Teólogos Españoles*, Vol.5, Salamanca 1934, p.155.

[6] The Authorized King James Version of Luke 6,35 as quoted in the text is in the same tradition of interpretation as that of the Vulgate, which reads: *Mutuum date, nihil inde sperantes.* There is another tradition according to which the original has the meaning corresponding to the Latin, *nihil desperantes*, i.e.: (Lend), *despairing* of nothing! This is in the spirit of carefree love of God and man which Christ preaches in the Sermon on the Mount, but it does not refer specifically to usury. It preaches charity in lending without distinguishing between principal and interest. The majority opinion among biblical scholars is reported to be that renunciation of both principal and interest is intended, in which case the verse can hardly be a precept but must be a counsel. The scholastics, following Aquinas, took it to be a counsel as to the principal and a precept as to interest (positively forbidding usury). Cf. O'Brien 166-7, with references.

much more of it is concerned either with interpretation and application of individual laws and paragraphs, or with induction of general principles *from* them, than with the justification of positive legislation on the basis of natural law, though something of this is to be found in the mature commentaries on the *Decretals*. On the whole, authors in this genre were as content with the authority of law as the theologians were with the authority of Scripture. More interesting from our point of view are the popular summaries for confessors. Often referring closely to canon law titles, these handbooks were written for the "internal" rather than the "external" forum. In the forum of conscience, natural law might forbid what positive law permitted.[7]

Natural law was also the law of reason. The scholastics were prepared to prove by rational argument that usury was wrong. Let us not fault them for trying to deduce value judgments without value premises; we are interested in their premises, however implicit and value-laden they were. Sometimes their premises turn out to be authority again, once or twice removed. Shortly before the close of the fifteenth century, the Heidelberg professor, Conrad Summenhart, launched the first broadside attack on scholastic usury doctrine. This important work cleared the path for further advances, both popular (like that of the reformer, Calvin) and academic (like that of Molinaeus, in

[7] In order to keep the list of sources quoted within reasonable limits, I shall make no attempt at all to trace the natural law case against usury through the commentary literature on the *Decretals* and refer instead quite generally to the bio-bibliographical section of Langholm (2). Two early works of this genre must be mentioned, however, viz. the commentary by Innocent IV (pope and canonist, d. 1254), quoted in the edition of Frankfurt 1570, and the *Summa aurea* on the *Decretals* by Hostiensis (Henry of Susa, d. 1271), Basel 1573. The greatest fourteenth-century canonist, Joannes Andreae (d. 1348), discusses usury most extensively in a book which is nominally a commentary on the *regulae iuris* of the *Sextum*. It consists of questions inspired by these rules and was popularly known as the *Quaestiones mercuriales*. Edition used: Lyon 1551. Summaries for confessors, quoted in articles on usury: Raymond of Peñafort (d. 1275), Rome 1603; Astesanus (d. 1330), Lyon 1519; Pisanus (Bartholomew of Pisa, d. 1347), Augsburg 1475; Angelus (of Chivasso, d. 1495), Rouen 1513; Baptista Trovamala (d. after 1494), Strasbourg 1516.

whom modern critics used to see their first spokesman). While presenting a conventional array of authorities stating that usury is against both divine and human canon law (with which he does not quarrel), Summenhart lists twenty-five different arguments alleged to have been advanced at one time or another to prove that it is against natural law. To these arguments he returns in the following chapter and starts to pick them to pieces, in the end rejecting all but three. These three must stand, says Summenhart (perhaps ironically), because they are supported by the authorities of Aristotle, Cicero and St Ambrose of Milan.[8] However, Summenhart's counter-case depends on how convincingly he reasons under twenty-two other headings. As it turns out, he encounters Aristotle under several of them.

Aristotle stands a little apart on the scholastic gallery of authorities. As a heathen, he could not claim the gift of revelation; if his utterances were true, they must be so on the strength of human reason alone. Note, says Olivi, concluding one of his arguments against usury, that Aristotle was decided in this solely by the reason of natural equity. If his reasoning tended to be taken on trust more than that of any other heathen, it was because he was *the Philosopher:* the first authority not only on the subject matters of philosophy, such as ethics and politics, but also on the art of philosophizing itself. Such trust in supreme reasoning power may be more destructive of thought

[8] *Tractatus de contractibus*, Questions 22 and 23, Venice 1580, pp.71-94. This is the recommended edition of Summenhart, but several early sixteenth-century editions made the work available to Calvin's generation. The author died in 1502. The best known early academic critic of scholastic usury doctrine used to be the French lawyer Charles Dumoulin (Molinaeus, d. 1566), whose treatise on contracts and usury is quoted here in the edition of Lyon 1558. We there find Summenhart lumped with the other scholastic "sophists", although Molinaeus makes good use of his counter-arguments. It has been suggested that Summenhart wrote with tongue in cheek when he wound up with a suggestion of conflict between reason and scriptural (with Aristotelian) authority. But to infer insincerity is a questionable critical principle. Most likely, Summenhart was sincerely puzzled. His conclusions may have paved the way for "moderate" usury, but his wrestling with the old arguments could also serve the further development of Aristotelian doctrine and was in fact used for that purpose: "Conradus" was much quoted at Salamanca.

than trust in any other kind of authority. This is the negative aspect of Aristotelianism and the grievance which post-scholastic critics have never tired of voicing. The positive aspect which perhaps more than balanced the account in the Middle Ages is the aid to reasoning which the Aristotelian system no doubt represented. However, it would seem that those who hung most closely on the lips of the Philosopher, viz. the textual commentators on his works, were not those in the best position to draw on this kind of aid; they were mostly content to interpret the unquestioned truth of his sayings. Those who disputed questions in ethics and politics on the basis of Aristotle, were better placed; but to find the most constructive development of his analysis we must draw even farther away from the intimidating presence, just as from legal and theological authority.[9]

In medieval as in modern literature, the place to look for the fullest and least biased treatment of any particular subject in moral and political philosophy would seem to be in treatises devoted specifically to that subject, viz., *in casu*, in treatises *De usuris*. There are not many works of that description extant from the period which mainly interests us here, but they do exist. Medieval literature was not *all* commentary. Topical treatises on mundane matters began to multiply already in the thirteenth

[9] The following textual commentaries on Aristotle's *Politics* are quoted: Albert the Great, in *Opera*, Vol.8, Paris 1891; Thomas Aquinas (breaking off in Book III), in *Opera*, Vol.48, Rome 1971 (a different *Opera* edition, with the best critical text of the Latin translation of Aristotle himself); Walter Burley (d. c. 1346, unprinted), Paris BMaz 3496; Guido Vernani (d. after 1344), Venice BMarc lat.VI,94; as well as a fourteenth-century anonymous commentary (Nicholas Trevet?) in Oxford BodL 292. An interesting tradition of commentary on the *Politics* in the form of questions is preserved in several related manuscripts, including one in Paris BN lat.16089 (ascribed to Peter of Auvergne, the continuator of Aquinas's textual commentary), and one in Bologna BU 1625. This tradition was picked up in the *Quaestiones* by John Buridan (d. after 1358) on the *Politics* as well as on the *Ethics*, both quoted in editions of Paris 1513. While commenting on the *Ethics*, Buridan also builds on the textual commentary (with questions) by Odonis, Brescia 1482. A further brief step removed from the classical texts are the medieval authors of political treatises, by far the most explicit and influential one as regards usury being Giles of Rome's *De regimine principum*. Edition consulted: Rome 1556.

century. In the case of economics, it must be admitted that much of this writing is somewhat dependent on (or at least biased in the direction of) either theology, law or Aristotelian philosophy, but there are also some contributions of this nature which approach fairly balanced positions, drawing profitably on all the textual traditions sketched above without being unduly drawn in by any one of them. It is by studying Aristotelian principles at work in books of this description that I believe we can get closer to certain essentials of usury theory. I propose to do this by utilizing more fully some neglected treatises on usury and by adding three treatises previously overlooked.

If these could be overlooked for so long it is partly because of a not unnatural overexposure of the peak figures of scholasticism (not always the best economists) at the cost of the army of supporters, and partly because of the accident of selective publishing during the early modern period, which still to some extent determines the availability of different kinds of sources. Thus, for instance, the enormous libraries of legal commentaries, much in demand in the sixteenth and seventeenth centuries, must account for some of the modern critical focus on scholastic casuistry. Similarly, the comprehensive *summae* of the remembered masters of theology would catch the attention of the early printer (and so of the modern medieval scholar) more readily than the occasional topical treatise, slimmer in total volume but often less summary and more competent in treatment of the particular subject in which its author has taken a special interest. As a matter of fact, it was sometimes a confusion or an association of its author with some more famous figure which saved such a work from oblivion.

A treatise *De usuris* used to be attributed to Thomas Aquinas and was in fact published among the latter's collected works even as late as in the nineteenth-century Parma edition, still in current use.[10] It was actually written shortly after Aquinas's death (the date has been estimated at between 1276 and 1285) by Giles of Lessines (d. after 1304), a fellow Dominican and

[10] Vol.17, Parma 1864.

student of Albert the Great. The mistaken identity of the author drew this work into the range of scholarly attention at an early date and imported some slight confusion into the picture of Aquinas's stand on usury, since some rather un-Thomist views are expressed in it. Until recently, this was confidently believed to be the only treatise on usury composed during the peak period of scholasticism. But it is not. Languishing in manuscript until 1962, an equally interesting and somewhat related work bearing the same title is now available in an excellent critical edition. This is the treatise by Alexander Lombard (of Alessandria in Piedmont), probably based on disputes held at Genoa in 1307 while Alexander, a Franciscan, was on his way to Paris to succeed John Duns Scotus as regent professor there. Later he was briefly general of his order until his death in 1314. The frequency of respectful references in subsequent works on usury proves Alexander Lombard to have been quite influential.[11] Like Giles of Lessines he uses Aristotle with confidence and skill.

This seemed to be all specifically about usury for a long time. After the lull in literary activity following the Black Death, there are several treatises *De contractibus*. As this title indicates, they deal with different kinds of economic contracts, and there is naturally a watch kept for usurious elements. Well known authors are Henry of Hassia (d. 1397), John Gerson (d. 1429), and John Nider (d. 1438). Summenhart's work continues this genre, which was to expand greatly in the final phase of scholasticism, into which we need not pursue it here. The fifteenth century also saw once again the publication of treatises specifying usury in their title. Some relate closely to legal sources and are less relevant. I mention only those by Lorenzo Ridolfi (d. 1442) and Antonio Roselli (d. 1466). Two Franciscan authors, Francis of Platea (d. 1460) and Alexander Ariosto (d. after 1484) are more balanced in regard to different traditions and may repay closer examination as source-books on the mature doctrine.[12] As such, however, they have been far outranked by the

[11] For the text of this treatise and information about the author, see Hamelin.

[12] Hassia is in Gerson's *Opera*, Vol.4, Cologne 1484 (another instance of survival by association). Gerson's own treatise was consulted in a later *Opera*

work which has been considered until now the supreme specimen of the genre and has figured prominently in all histories of usury teaching since Werner Sombart entered this field.

Intent on disproving Max Weber's ideas about the confessional concomitants of early capitalism, Sombart pointed to two "pious gentlemen" who had "developed the concept of capital to a fine point", namely the Franciscan preacher, Bernardino of Siena (1380-1444) and the Dominican archbishop of Florence, Antonino Pierozzi (1389-1459),[13] "the two great economic thinkers of the Middle Ages", as Raymond de Roover was later to call them in a book subtitle.[14] Antonino of Florence is the less interesting of the two from our present point of view. What positive arguments he states against usury are taken from Bernardino or from sources already utilized more fully by him. However, they were both immensely influential. Bernardino of Siena wrote a series of sermons on economic subjects which were printed separately as a treatise on contracts in 1474.[15] Antonino was the author of a monumental *Summa theologica*.[16] Both treat closely and extensively of usury. Through the late fifteenth-century treatises cited above and through the frequently published summaries for the confessional written by friars, as well as through other channels, they dominated the analysis of usury as continued by the later scholastics, for instance in the Salamanca tradition.

What made these authors trump cards in Sombart's hand is

edition, viz. Antwerp 1706, Vol.3,1. Nider's *Tractatus de contractibus mercatorum*, appearing at Cologne about 1468, is believed to be the first economic treatise ever to be printed. Ridolfi and Roselli are (with much similar material) in *Tractatus universi iuris*, Vol.7, Venice 1584. The following were read in incunabula editions: Platea, *Opus restitutionum, usurarum et excommunicationum*, Venice 1472; Ariosto, *Tractatus usurarum*, Bologna 1486.

[13] Sombart 320-1. In a long counter-critical note to Sombart, even Weber (197) must admit that Bernardino and Antonino were "relatively friendly to capital".

[14] De Roover was made aware of Bernardino's debt to Olivi (42 with note 220). It is unfortunate that this scholar (who did so much to improve our understanding of medieval economics) was unable to follow up that important lead.

[15] Thus narrowly beaten to the book of records by Nider and Platea. The authoritative edition of these sermons is now *Opera*, Vol.4, Quaracchi (Florence) 1956.

[16] Edition used: Verona 1740.

the fact that the process of exemption from the general ban on usury in their works was so far advanced. They are unquestionably exponents of orthodox Catholic doctrine. It is true that Bernardino was somewhat involved in the continuous struggle over the adherence to the Franciscan Rule, which might cause his name to be associated with a class of rebels, but those were rebels hardly deviating in the direction of economic leniency. Antonino was highly placed in the ecclesiastical hierarchy and was a faithful Thomist. And yet these men show that they have a lot of understanding for the position of the creditor and speak of *capital* in a remarkably modern way. No one had heard scholastics speak like that before. Numerous critics have returned to these works and they have tended to confuse the Weber issue not a little. The question of what historical factors gave rise to a "spirit of capitalism" in the early modern era clearly permitted of different solutions. Perhaps the discovery of Bernardino and Antonino tended to score the best point to those who favoured materialistic rather than confessional or intellectual interpretations. After all, what is it that speaks in these authors but the commercial conditions of the early North Italian urban Renaissance? It must have been able to anticipate subsequent universal developments by a century or so.

Nevertheless, Bernardino of Siena is an Aristotelian. He accepts the basic principles of the *Politics*. The fruits justly reaped by the agents of capitalistic enterprise, according to him, can always be attributed to other factors and must always be justified under "extrinsic titles" – extrinsic, that is, to money, which can bear no fruit. Bernardino accepts no "moderate" usury justifiable as a normal market estimate of the value of the use of money as such; the idea would be unthinkable. Other crucial arguments later to be rejected by Summenhart and the Protestant apologists are also still vigorously supported by the Franciscan preacher. What makes his teaching look new is analytical as much as doctrinal. The old arguments are not given exactly the same content as when the first generation of Aristotelians stated them, nor does the proposition that money is barren mean exactly what it meant then. There is a kind of integrated argumentation in Bernardino, by which the mutually supporting arguments reduce to the same principle. By this principle, "reasonable" lenders' claims can be met while usury is still a sin against justice.

It is not surprising that this analysis (and some equally remarkable contributions to value theory contained in the same volume) should cause Bernardino to be reputed a great economist in the judgment of historians, however unlikely a figure he may have seemed for such a distinction. Ideas will naturally be attributed to those in whom immediate posterity seeks authority for them, which in this case meant Bernardino and to some extent Antonino of Florence. Moreover, research in anterior sources revealed little to account for them in the various commentary traditions sketched above. On the other hand, Bernardino was evidently a great quoter (often but not always naming his sources), and one might perhaps have suspected that some analytical development had been going on before him. It is owing mainly to the painstaking research of the Quaracchi editors of Bernardino's *Opera* that this can be shown to be correct. Just as the authors of economic treatises after Bernardino tend to rely on him, so he utilizes to the full some previous treatises. In fact, nearly all there is of positive economic analysis in Bernardino of Siena is borrowed from earlier authors. Among them are both Giles of Lessines and Alexander Lombard. But three other authors, writing in the same general period, provide the essence of his Aristotelian analysis.

In the medieval city of Siena a thoroughfare appropriately named the Street of Wisdom (*Via della Sapienza*) leads to the library which preserves the most fascinating pair of volumes in the early history of economics. They are in manuscript and contain the treatises on buying and selling, usury and restitution by two Franciscan friars, Peter (Pierre de Jean) Olivi and Gerald Odonis, both works annotated in the hand of Bernardino of Siena. The same old library possesses one of the few extant copies of the single printed edition of a treatise on usury written by another native of that city, namely the Augustinian, Gerardo of Siena. These three authors, then, were all friars, had all studied at Paris in their youth, and had a common centre of gravity in the Mediterranean area. Alexander Lombard fits this description as well (as do Aquinas and other key contributors to usury theory). It was on an integrated Mediterranean analytic tradition that Bernardino drew. Written in the decades following the death of Aquinas, when the ancient sources were familiar and the immediate task of annotation and comparison was done, it is not too much to say that the collected contribution of these unusually perceptive masters represents the culmination of medieval economic analysis as well as the momentum for much subsequent development. In the case of Olivi and Odonis, this is true of the analysis of commodity exchange and value as well as of usury.

A brief and in outward appearances not very happy life but a lasting influence was granted the Franciscan theologian Olivi, of Sérignan (on the coast east of Narbonne), who was accused of heresy and came to be associated with the Spiritual faction of his order. He lectured at Montpellier and Narbonne, where he died in 1298 at the age of fifty. In the 1280's he also lectured briefly at Florence. His economic treatise is a relatively late work and may have been written there; anyhow, all extant copies of it have come to light in Italy. It is actually a triple treatise. The first part, dealing with buying and selling and never printed before, recently appeared in a critical edition with an Italian translation. It presents us with the original version of the analysis for which Bernardino of Siena was long held in high repute as a theorist of value and price. The second and third parts are not included in this edition, but they have been printed a number of times before, first at Rome in 1556 and last at Bologna i 1671. These editions are rare; moreover, they appear under a false name, namely that of Gerardo of Siena. Consequently, Olivi was an author as forgotten in usury theory as in value theory, until Bernardino's marginal notes were discovered in the Siena manuscript of the treatise and his extensive borrowings from Olivi became evident. The part on usury consists of a single question, with a number of *dubia*. It runs into some eight thousand words, approximately two thirds of which are copied, with only small variations but in many scattered fragments, into the economic sermons of the fifteenth-century preacher. These loans are nowhere acknowledged.[17]

Just one item removed from Olivi on the shelves of the Siena library is a similar treatise by Gerald Odonis, whom Bernardino need not be afraid to quote. (In fact, he does quote him occasionally under the name of Giraldus, whom some critics took to be Gerardo of Siena, making the confusion complete.) Born at Camboulit, near Figeac, Odonis taught at Toulouse and later became a widely travelled man on papal missions, a general of his order, a bishop and patriarch. He died in Sicily in 1349. Odonis is known as a writer on philosophy mainly because of his commentary on the *Nicomachean Ethics.* A man of analytical acumen but a quarrelsome mind (a not unusual combination), Odonis commented on Aristotle with an eye on Aquinas, from whom he suggests some fruitful departures in the chapter on economic exchange in Book V. He also discusses money there, and thus contributes to the tradition on the value of money and on debasement which passes through Buridan to Nicole Oresme. The form chosen by Odonis is a textual exposition with questions. In a question in Book IV (also picked up by Buridan) he discusses usury. In treating of these various subjects Odonis depends on Olivi, just as he does in his own economic treatise. This treatise, probably composed before the commentary, can in fact be read in part as a paraphrase of Olivi's work. But Odonis quarrels with Olivi as well. Thus he deepens the former's value analysis. In one of the most rewarding discussions in the part about usury he takes Olivi systema-

[17] On Olivi's life and ideas, see Bettoni. On the treatise utilized by Bernardino of Siena, and its strange publishing history, see Pacetti and Cuyás. The part about exchange and value, with the translation and a doctrinal study, is in Spicciani. These are the four editions of the part about usury, all in the name of Gerardo of Siena: Rome 1556 (Ravenna BClass – plus half a dozen other copies), Viterbo 1587 (Perugia BC – only copy known to me), Bologna 1626 (Rome BAng, Milan BN), Bologna 1671 (BVat – another half dozen copies). Olivi also composed *Quodlibeta* consulted by Bernardino. They were published at Venice about 1505 and will merit a single reference below. Unless otherwise indicated, all references will be to the treatise in the manuscript which contains Bernardino's personal notes, viz. Siena BC U.V.6.

tically to task for his arguments based on natural law. But this criticism is no more destructive of Aristotelian principles as such, than is Odonis's criticism of Aquinas. Unlike the *Ethics* commentary, the treatise on usury and other economic matters was never printed and survives precariously only in the Siena manuscript. When references to it crop up in fifteenth-century works, transmission must be traced through Bernardino of Siena.[18]

The last work to be mentioned in this literary sketch, and the one with which the works of both Olivi and Odonis have sometimes been confused, is the treatise on usury and prescriptions by the Augustinian friar, Gerardo of Siena. This author's life seems to have been rather less eventful than those of either of the other two, but he was a highly respected master, well versed in theology, philosophy and canon law. Having studied at Paris like them, he returned to teach in the convents of his order at Bologna and later at his native Siena. One of the three extant copies of Olivi's treatise has come to light in each of these cities, where Gerardo may have had access to it. While dates of composition cannot be ascertained with precision in any of the three cases, it is reasonable to believe that Gerardo of Siena occupied a middle chronological position and there is some internal evidence to indicate that he did in fact know Olivi's work. He may have died as late as 1336 but is reported to have lived into old age and his literary career probably spanned the first two decades of the fourteenth century. Joannes Andreae, the famous canonist, informs us that one of his teachers, who died in 1313, had used Gerardo. As for his position on the traditional arguments against usury, Gerardo can often be seen to agree with a better known Augustinian master, namely Giles of Rome, whom he may have consulted. The treatise on usury was printed once, at Cesena in 1630, but this edition is also rare and has never to my knowledge been used before as a literary source for the history of economics. The ideas expressed in it

[18] On Odonis's *Ethics* commentary, see Langholm (1) with bio-bibliographical information. For edition used, see note 9 above. The economic treatise is in Siena BC U.V.8. Unless otherwise indicated, references are to this manuscript.

are regularly attributed to Andreae, who reproduced Gerardo's arguments with only minor reservations, and to Bernardino of Siena, who used both sources. Some of the most important reconstructions of usury theory on Aristotelian bases are due to Gerardo of Siena and spread through these channels.[19]

Bernardino of Siena's analysis of usury (as distinct from his preaching and some of his casuistry) is a patchwork of many sources. For the lines of analysis to be traced in this study he reaches all the way back to the treatises described above. It must place Bernardino's relevance to the discussion around the Weber thesis in a new light to learn that even the defences of the creditor's concern for his capital, which so shocked and delighted scholars, are verbatim borrowings. These are not even Catholic Renaissance sentiments, but echoes of a far-off medieval voice. There ought to be a lesson in this. Taken out of historical (and literary) context, ideological overtones can be read into these statements, because one is listening for them, which in the true context must vanish. In the course of the following chapters we shall have occasion to quote some of the statements which were made to sound sensational when issuing from the pens of Bernardino and Antonino, along with numerous other statements which they quoted from Olivi, Odonis and Gerardo of Siena. In no way do they foreshadow the breakdown of Aristotelian ideology. The remarkable thing is that they contain Aristotelian analysis sufficiently advanced to be unsuspectingly postdated by scholars by a century and more. To know this must unfortunately reduce Bernardino and Antonino to rather pale copiers. On the other hand it must greatly enhance the analytical stature of the men with whom these ideas originated.

[19] One must have recourse to lexica, old and new, for information about Gerardo of Siena. There are notes or articles in Diplovataccius (*Iur. cons.*, 1968) 259; Gandolfus (*Diss.*, 1704) 135-6; Glorieux (*Litt. quodl.*,II, 1935) 97-8; Hurter (*Nomenclator*,II, 1906) 542-3; Ossinger (*Bibl. Aug.*, 1786) 827-9; Perini (*Bibl. Aug.*,III, 1935) 187-9; Potthast (*Repertorium emendatum et auctum*,IV, 1976) 700; etc. I used a copy of the Cesena edition of Gerardo's treatise in the Biblioteca Angelica (T-4-5), where it is bound with a very rare copy of the first Bologna edition of Olivi. This library also possesses the only known copy of the manuscript of Gerardo from which the edition was made (Cod. 625).

2. The equitable contract

Albert the Great, the universal doctor and teacher of all Latin Aristotelians, commented twice on the *Nicomachean Ethics*. The ink was hardly dry on the parchment of Robert Grosseteste's Latin translation when Albert lectured on it at Cologne. Thomas Aquinas was in the audience and later helped his master edit the work, which mostly takes the form of a close textual exposition. Ideas capable of firing the imaginations of generations of subsequent commentators glitter throughout it. Years later, after an interval of preaching and administration, the ageing Albert wrote a different kind of commentary, not so much in order to correct or improve on his explanations in detail as to place Aristotle's teaching in the broader perspective of scholastic philosophy. In Book V of the *Ethics* there is a chapter which came to rank prominently among the *loci communes* of the medieval economists. It discusses the principles of equivalence in the exchange of commodities, with or without the medium of money.[1] The context is justice, so this is where the scholastics went to consult Aristotle on "the just price". However, if modern scholars had read carefully Albert the Great's introduction to this chapter, some confusion about the nature of the medieval just price might have been avoided.

Several pages in advance, and again just before drawing the Aristotelian diagram of equivalence, Albert in his second commentary cites Cicero in *De inventione* on the triple base of validity in customary law, namely by equity, covenant and decision (*par, pactum, et iudicatum*). In Cicero's own words,

[1] 1132b-1133b.

A covenant (*pactum*) is an agreement between some persons. Equity (*par*) is what is just and fair to all. A decision (*iudicatum*) is something determined previously by the opinion of some person or persons.[2]

These different principles, says Albert the Great, can all be seen in operation in the market-place. Sometimes, for the good of the community, the sovereign will decree a maximum price, for instance in order to limit the damaging effects of scarcity. Sometimes terms of exchange are determined by the parties themselves. If free of deception such agreements are valid even if strict equivalence does not obtain. Finally, terms of exchange are sometimes made to comply with equivalence or parity in the strict sense.[3] This is what Aristotle calls *contrapassum* (reciprocity), which Albert then proceeds to discuss, repeating and extending criteria suggested in his first commentary.

The reference to Cicero, no less than the Aristotelian context itself, poses the question of economic ethics as envisaged here by Albert the Great squarely within the compass of justice rather than charity. This is the frame of reference which is to be maintained in the present study, even as we proceed from the purchase of commodities to the borrowing of money. It is a frame of reference peculiar to the scholastics, which must be kept in mind, since usury originally was, and later again became, a sin against charity, where justice could raise no arm against it. Needless to say, even in the age of the just price, the moralist would preach the charitable price, and the two aspects of scholastic doctrine are not always easily separable. It is not to be denied that considerations of Christian virtues alien both to the Greek and to the Roman can often be sensed behind what is taught within the legal framework, such as when cheating those in particular need of our compassion is judged more harshly. However (and this is what counts here), the system sketched in the ancient terms quoted above was capable of being so adjusted as to arrest many abuses of this kind on its own terms.

The relationship between precepts of positive and of natural

[2] *De inventione*,II,liv; Hubbell's translation; Loeb Classical Library, No.386, pp.328-331; cf. Albert, *Opera*, Vol.7 (Paris 1891), p.350.

[3] Albert, op.cit., p.355.

law was touched upon briefly in the preceding chapter and need occupy us little more here, provided it is recognized that a notable fraction of economic contracts in the Middle Ages was determined *ad iudicatum*. If this is taken to include rates and prices based on custom and community consensus, the part of the economy which was thus regulated was probably larger then than it is even in some of the closely regulated economies of Western Europe today. The medieval just price was therefore frequently simply an official price, probably more often established by some corporation than by Albert's sovereign. The scholastic economists were on the whole disinclined to dispute either the fact or the substance of this kind of regulations. On the contrary, they welcomed such regulations and gladly saw them extended. Their task, as they conceived of it, was not to improve on the economic system, of which they could have only the haziest notion, but rather to improve on individual human relations within any system instituted by God. If the task of establishing and enforcing reasonable exchange relations was taken out of their hands by the secular authorities, so much the better. On the other hand, there was nothing Hobbesian about their attitude to positive law. It was understood that the requirements maintained in the internal forum of conscience might be stricter than those maintained in the external forum of the courts; just as, in the former forum, charity might counsel where justice could not command. This was very evident in the case of usury, which positive law to some extent did, and indeed must, tolerate.

In the case of commodity exchange, just as in the case of the lending and borrowing of money, officially determined rates may issue from considerations different from those underlying ethical norms of equivalence between individual contracting parties. Prices set *ad iudicatum* therefore represent one material contraction of the domain of what is conventionally thought of as medieval just price doctrine proper. But its area of application was even narrower than that, for the scholastic economists hardly aspired to regulating all exchanges not subject to official price determination. Historians of economics have differed greatly in their interpretations of the criteria on which just equivalence was supposed to be established. At one time, different schools sprang up, defending fundamentally opposing views regarding this question. In consequence, an undue amount of attention has focused on it. Some of the criteria examined in the course of this long debate were economic criteria proper, such as cost or market estimates; some were social criteria, such as "status" or whatever. Some interpreters even went so far as to suggest that the principle of equivalence was to be sought in the intrinsic nature of the goods themselves, based on purely metaphysical considerations.

The worst of these misconceptions are now weeded out, but there still lingers in conventional history books the impression that the establishment of such a criterion was mainly what scholastic economics was about. It is as though its whole aim was to find some exact, universal formula: exact in the sense that it was capable of fixing just terms of exchange with precision, and universal in the sense that it was to be applied to all exchanges. But if there was one idea which the scholastics would have shunned, it was this one. Their just price criteria were far from exact; on the contrary, they were rough rules of thumb, allowing for variations within wide limits of tolerance. This is something the scholastics themselves were careful to emphasize. Moreover, the different criteria were mutually supporting rather than conflicting. The conflict between a labour and a market criterion, for instance, on which much of the critical debate centred, was read into the historical context by post-Ricardian economists. Most important of all, these criteria were meant to apply only by exception. In any society permitting some freedom of bargaining, the vast majority of terms concluded *ad pactum* between individual parties must be allowed to pass without the moralist interfering. Terms established *ad par*, viz. terms of "just price" in the conventional sense, binding in the forum of conscience, went into operation only in such exceptional cases as when disputes had to be settled, when conscientious exchangers sought guidance, when terms of restitution for sinful gains had to be suggested, etc.

In such instances, just price computations might serve one of two purposes. They might serve as *correctives* to the price agreed upon when conditions of free bargaining were violated, issuing in patently unreasonable terms. Alternatively, they might serve as *checks* on actual terms to indicate whether conditions of free bargaining were in fact operative. The presence of a third person may not be required to constitute this kind of check and effect this kind of corrective. Knowledge of what one's confessor considers to be rules of *par* may (hopefully) influence exchangers about to conclude a *pactum*. However much the cynical historian will discount such indirect effects of just price doctrine, they cannot have been entirely negligible. On the other hand, such general guidance is insufficient when exchangers disagree as to what price and what other terms of contract best fulfil the requirements of justice under certain particular circumstances. The task of the moralist, therefore, is not only to suggest criteria but to apply them to cases.

Scholastic economic ethics as a system can then also be viewed from two different angles. From the conventional angle it looks like a set of criteria by which *par* is to be estimated. If the system is turned around it may appear as a set of criteria by which to judge the validity of *pactum*. The two viewpoints are mutually illuminating. Considering the predominance of the former viewpoint in existing literature on the subject I might suggest that future researchers could profitably forget about the nature of the "just price" for a while and rather concentrate on the principles conditioning the bargaining process as formulated by the medieval canonists and philosophers. However, both approaches are necessary in order to fully explore the doctrine. The dominant presence of Aristotle is soon encountered however one starts. The conventional approach leads to Aristotle on *reciprocity* in *Ethics*, V (being the context introduced by Albert the Great as quoted above). The alternative approach will take us to Aristotle on the nature of *consent* in *Ethics*, III. I have examined some Aristotelian sources and suggested some general conclusions about scholastic economic ethics as viewed from these alternative angles in two previous works.[4] My aim here is merely to review and relate these previous findings so far as is required for a proper understanding of the place of usury in the overall doctrine.

Granted that official prices and rates make a certain inroad into the operation of just price estimates, it is natural to ask next what is actually left for such estimates to regulate when freedom of bargaining is accepted as the general rule in cases where the secular authorities are silent. In other words, when does a contract valid in positive law violate moral criteria? Clearly, the answer to this question in any society at any point in time will reflect a basic attitude to economic liberalism as a moral code. If one were to follow the development of economic ethics from late medieval through Renaissance to early modern principles, I suggest that the waning of scholastic (and indeed of Catholic) influences can be measured by the increasing preparedness to accept terms of exchange established *ad pactum* at the cost of those which had to be reviewed *ad par.* In the middle of the seventeenth century, Thomas Hobbes openly ridiculed Aristotelian equivalence as a relevant concept of commutative justice. The just value of a thing contracted for, said Hobbes, is measured by the appetite of the contractors and expressed in the price which they agree upon. Justice, as a technical term, can refer only to the *performance* of covenant, not to the *terms* of covenant.[5]

Choice vouches for consent and consent vouches for justice. If you have agreed to pay a certain price, you should be held to your promise by the forces of law and morality; what made you agree in the first place is a psychological not a moral question. Being "free to choose" (as a current idiom has it) whether to accept or reject the terms offered, you have no cause of complaint. It is true that Leviathan himself may descend on the market-place and restrict your operations, but *iudicatum* and *pactum* between them entirely eliminate the domain of *par.* Hobbes is one philosopher who thrived by overstatement and must suffer the fate of being quoted to mark extreme positions.

[4] Cf. Langholm (1) and (2).

[5] *Leviathan*,I,15.

Nevertheless, there is some truth to the proposition that the philosophical tradition which reached the classical economists in a line from Hobbes through Locke and Hume did not possess an ethic in terms of justice. Transgressions of rules governing private agreements are taken care of entirely by positive law. It was up to Christian charity to soften this harsh doctrine, and it should not be forgotten, in the case of these authors, that if they reduced the virtue of justice to a powerless formalism, they nearly always did appeal to the virtue of charity for material support. Thus they may have believed that they preserved ethical content where they abandoned ethical form. This I believe to be a delusion. At any rate, on this point, a particular formal structure was essential to the scholastic paradigm.

The political philosophers of the seventeenth and eighteenth centuries are transitional figures. Since this makes it possible to read them as anticipators, they are often viewed in a perspective which points forward, towards the social sciences of our own times. This may unfortunately obscure the fact that these authors are frequently quoted in polemical works marking the termination of traditions which extend backwards through the scholastic centuries. What speaks in Hobbes as quoted above is an extreme interpretation of the economic liberalism of the Roman law, finally triumphant, and directed against a system of restriction and modification constructed by medieval civilians and canonists and adopted by the scholastic economists. The three fundamental principles supporting economic liberalism in Roman law are (1) that anybody is moderator and arbiter of his own good[6] (which would seem to imply that he may keep it or sell it as he pleases and demand any price he likes), (2) that a willing party is not injured[7] (implying that once a price is willingly agreed upon, the legal issue is closed), and (3) that, consequently, "a thing is worth what it can be sold for".[8] The

[6] Code 4,35,21; cf. 4,38,14.

[7] Digest 39,3,9,1; cf. 47,10,1,5.

[8] In the early glosses, as invited by the text at Digest 9,2,33; 35,2,63, and elsewhere. For further particulars and references concerning the matters discussed on the following four pages, see Langholm (2).

latter sounds familiar; it is how economists still define value in exchange. But no well-ordered modern society would be prepared to accept these legal maxims as they stand, and no more did the scholastics. Positive law will set some strict limits to their operation, as did secular and ecclesiastical law in the Middle Ages. In addition (and this is what marks the difference from what came later), the scholastic moralists, writing for the internal forum of human conscience, would like to control these principles more strictly than the external courts were inclined to do. They would see transgressions as a moral issue, in terms of justice. By and large, however, the moralists could build on the system of restrictions developed by the lawyers. It is this extended system which appears when scholastic economic ethics is viewed as a set of criteria by which to judge the validity of individual economic agreements.

A thing is worth what it can be sold for, said the great fourteenth century civilian Bartolus, provided the buyer *knows what he buys.*[9] This modification is capable of extension in several dimensions carefully and thoroughly explored by the Bartolists. Many of their findings are still with us. Fraud is ruled out, and there is a whole literature on what kinds of withholding of information amount to fraud and on the extent of *caveat emptor.* By the same token (or at least by refashioning it slightly so as to make insufficient information encompass insufficient capacity for receiving information), exploitation of immature and mentally incapacitated buyers (or sellers as the case may be) is also ruled out. The buyer must know *and understand* what he buys. What underlies these rulings is a principle absolutely fundamental in European legal thought, namely that validity of contract presumes *consent.* No one can be said to consent to terms of exchange which he does not know or understand. This immediately leads to an association with force (coercion, duress), which in some forms invalidates contracts immediately. A commodity is clearly not worth what it can only be sold for when the buyer is induced by threat of physical

[9] Bartolus on Digest 13,1,14; 36,1,1,16, and elsewhere.

injury to accept it on those terms. The same is true of blackmail and various forms of moral coercion. This kind of conditioning seems irrelevant to economics. We leave it to criminal law and take it for granted.

But the scholastics were not as yet prepared to leave the issue of force there. Violation of consent, by which a contract is rendered invalid, is possible whenever one party to the contract is in the power of the other party. While economists can ignore coercion by physical and moral power, there remains a kind of power which is *sui generis* to economics itself, the power which is the very operating force of economic systems. *Value is power,* as the early economists saw clearly. It is purchasing power which determines price in any individual exchange relation and in any market, if left to itself. The liberalistic tradition has conditioned us to think of such power as a property right violating no one, but this is conventional (and convenient) thinking. The scholastics saw it with fresher eyes. Coercion rendering contracts invalid to them might include *economic coercion* as a particular kind, different from but on a par with moral and physical coercion. If one party to a contract was in the *economic power* of the other party and this power was wielded in order to obtain unjust terms of exchange, the terms did not stand.

In working out their dialectic on economic coercion, the scholastics were guided by Aristotle's discussion of the *voluntary* in Book III of the *Ethics.* The classical context is man's moral responsibility for actions performed under duress. In this connection, Aristotle takes particular cognizance of a type of situation where an agent may be said to act willingly within the limits of choice imposed by circumstances but unwillingly in so far as acceptance of these strictures is concerned. Such situations are mixed as far as voluntariness is concerned, says Aristotle, citing the example of a ship's captain abandoning cargo to stay afloat.[10] This became a favourite locus of authority for the principle of *conditional consent.* The scholastic economists turned Aristotle's context around and applied his distinc-

[10] 1110a.

tion to the moral responsibility of agents exploiting duress imposed on others.

Recognizing that economic duress can influence price even in the absence of fraud and force in the legal sense, the scholastics would concede no difference in principle between taking advantage of duress and actively applying duress. The distinction between *compulsion* by impersonal force of circumstances and *coercion* by a human agent (on which the modern libertarian relies) was irrelevant to Aristotle's own discussion of the principles of responsibility. The scholastics, adopting Aristotle and examining the problem from the point of view of the oppressor, were disinclined to make any such distinction as might relieve a contracting party from blame by reference to economic conditions imposed by suprapersonal forces. The clue to scholastic ethics in questions like this is that its focus was on individual human relations not on social aggregates. They were *micro*-economists in the narrowest sense. There are historical reasons for this. It was a patristic inheritance, and perhaps the only possible moral focus in the unstructured world of the Dark Ages. Even in the fourteenth century, the social implications of economic behaviour were only very vaguely understood. Some economic phenomena can come to look quite different from this personalistic point of view. What we think of as impersonal value in exchange, expressed as general purchasing power, becomes the aggregate expression of the application of individual power. While the seller *can*, by force of circumstances, drive the price up to its value (which is the highest price at which it *can* be sold), he does not *have* to do so. He meets his brother in the context of exchange and the price demanded is in the final analysis subject to his own decision, for which he is morally responsible, whatever power the situation lends him. If economic coercion influences the terms of exchange, it is always to some extent personal coercion.

The scholastic economists thus faced a dilemma of their own making, namely to decide when terms of exchange entered upon are truly voluntary and thus valid and when consent is conditioned by force of circumstances. Let it be immediately admitted that the solution of the problem cannot be reduced to strict logic. We are never absolutely "free to choose"; in some way or other, we shall always want to see our range of alternatives extended and we can frequently point to individuals in a position to extend them for us. On the other hand, there is always some freedom of choice. A man walks to prison voluntarily, said Hobbes, in so far as he chooses to walk rather than being trailed along the ground. The fact that he would have preferred to walk off some place else, does not alter this fact. Similarly, a buyer is free to buy or not to buy, given the price offered, though he would have preferred the price to be lower. A borrower pays usury willingly in preference to being without money, but his consent is always conditional only, for he would rather have had the use of money for free. This double face of the situation is universal.[11] So where is the line to be drawn between cases of absolute and conditional consent? There is no answer to this except to point out that the scholastics here discussed ethics, not logic, and that they may therefore have been justified in thinking that they needed no hard and fast line. It was sufficient for them to make some rough distinctions between classes of goods (thus, for instance, weeding out luxuries as less worthy of protection) and to focus on some rough circumstantial characteristics as likely to indicate that a contracting party was placed under true economic compulsion not to be exploited. We need not go into this in detail here. Suffice it to say that such considerations are evidence of a concept of economic compulsion in a substantive not merely a formal sense. It turned on poverty, want and despair. Such qualities disappear in statistical demand schedules but are real enough for all that and are legitimate concerns of economic ethics.

The limitations thus imposed on free bargaining, as well as the criteria of just price to be applied as checks and correctives, are analysed with exceptional acuteness by Peter Olivi, the author on whom Bernardino of Siena relied more fully than any

[11] This logical defect in the scholastic model was pointed out already by Summenhart, who remarked that even the just price is sometimes paid unwillingly in Aristotle's absolute sense (*De contractibus*, Q.23, ad 14, p.91).

other for his own discussion of exchange. Olivi's treatise on buying and selling, which precedes the treatise on usury, consists of seven questions, some of them patterned on Thomas Aquinas's articles on buying and selling in the *Summa theologiae* (in the question preceding the Saint's treatment of usury) and bearing traces of the doctrinal influence of Henry of Ghent. But there is a peculiar sense of empiricism in Olivi lacking in these and most previous authors on the subject. One cannot doubt that he had been in the markets and inns where merchants argued. In his first two questions Olivi asks (1) whether a commodity may licitly be sold for more than its worth or bought for less, and (2) whether a commodity can be priced according to its use value to the buyer.[12] Cut up and rearranged with other material, these questions are copied almost to a word in Articles 1 and 2 of Bernardino's thirty-fifth economic sermon.[13]

Olivi's teaching must be taken to presuppose the general prevalence of free bargaining, which he seems to have favoured more wholeheartedly than most of his contemporaries. When adults of a sound mind, in the absence of fraud and force, agree on a price, that price is *eo ipso* just and valid. Arguing rhetorically in opposition to his own negative conclusion regarding the first question posed, he assumes the role of spokesman for the liberalistic position with ease and conviction, defending it in terms which have a surprisingly modern flavour to them. I can put any price I want on my own goods, says Olivi speaking as merchant; no law compels me to give up my own goods at a price which does not please me, just as the buyer is not compelled to buy if the price does not please him. Buying and selling are voluntary acts; hence pricing is voluntary, according to the rule that a thing is worth what it can be sold for. Moreover, the common good takes precedence over the private good. Among sinful men there is no exact way of pricing commodities in exchange, but a price established on the basis of free bargaining between buyer and seller expresses the common consent of both.

[12] Siena BC U.V.6, ff.295ra-297ra; ed Spicciani, pp.253-260.

[13] Pp.190-9.

It is the three Roman law maxims cited above which speak here; but for all his sympathy with them, Olivi cannot condone them unconditionally. The owner's right to dispose of his property as he pleases, says the author in reply, is restricted by the rules of just pricing once the commodities are actually offered in exchange, and justice is not sufficiently vouched for by the buyer's consent, which may be invalidated on account of ignorance and inexperience, or by some kind of compelling necessity. In the body of the question, stating his own positive teaching, Olivi says much the same thing in slightly different words: Terms of contract are valid unless consent issues from such feebleness of mind or from such duress as to rob them of legal force, or otherwise if consent is given owing to such poverty or other necessity that it cannot be said to express free will. In such cases the price agreement does not stand if the commodity is sold for more than its worth.

The very phrasing of Olivi's first question implies a rejection of the maxim that a thing is worth what it can be sold for, for the question would be meaningless in the absence of a different concept of "worth" against which actual sales could be measured to check and correct the bargaining process. Olivi does not propose a positive theory of value. In answering this first question he may seem to favour a market estimate of the just price. The body of the question contains a brief catalogue of factors influencing market value. They were to reach fame as Bernardino's *raritas* (scarcity), *virtuositas* and *complacibilitas* (roughly: objective and subjective utility). Discussed extensively in his Sermon 35, these catchwords originated (as still to be seen in Bernardino's Siena copy of Olivi's treatise) as marginalia to a similar discussion in Olivi. But the demand theorist who hopes to find a convinced antecedent in the thirteenth-century friar is soon disillusioned, for the body of the following question provides a rather different list of just price criteria. It also includes utility and scarcity, but leans more heavily on the cost side, suggesting labour, risk, industry, and productive skill. Bernardino of Siena copied all of this as well.

Olivi knew his Aristotle well, and his catalogues clearly reach back to the analysis of justice in exchange in Book V of the *Ethics*. In their attempts to explain this difficult section of text, the commentators in the course of the scholastic tradition introduced a number of suggestions similar to those extracted from Olivi above. Cost and market were present from the start. It was Albert the Great in his first commentary who suggested that equivalence in exchange could be measured on the basis of labour and production cost, while Thomas Aquinas more strongly accentuated relative utility as expressed by the exchanging parties' needs for each other's products. This eventually merged with the general acceptance of the competitive market price criterion of the just price, as the Aristotelian commentators in the tradition of Buridan developed a concept of effective demand on the basis of Aquinas.

Starting in the late nineteenth century, scholars looking back on Aristotelian economics from opposite camps of a modern ideological conflict, were bound to see the suggestions of Albert the Great and Thomas Aquinas as mutually exclusive and conflicting as well. The latter's position (always in the focus of attention) became a main bone of contention, for Aquinas remained a faithful disciple of the mentor of his youth and once or twice referred to labour himself. Perhaps this fact ought to have woken critics to their mistake, for the angelic doctor did not often contradict himself. In point of fact, the cost and market explanations travelled peacefully together through the scholastic tradition, supporting one another as estimates of fairness when possible. Elsewhere I even suggested that the persistent juxtaposition of these alternative ways of estimating the just price may have managed to impress on some scholastics a glimpse of the fact that cost and market price in the long run must tend to the same level.[14] If there is any merit to this suggestion (and I still believe that there is), then Olivi may partly be to thank for it. It was Aristotelians in the commentary tradition of Gerald Odonis who were best positioned for this

[14] For this and other points regarding Aristotle's exchange model mentioned below, see further Langholm (1).

important theoretical insight. As we know, Odonis had read Olivi's treatise on commodity exchange and usury and had written a critical paraphrase of it. Commenting on the *Nicomachean Ethics*, he brought some of Olivi's balanced analysis of value to the explanation of Aristotle as well.

The modern scholarly conflict between the cost and market interpretations of Aristotle's justice in exchange does not speak in very complimentary terms of the level of textual criticism in the history of economics. It must be mentioned here merely because it throws some light on a phase in the critical history of usury doctrine. Before we come to this, however, there is a different relationship between the cost and the market estimates which demands our attention in some detail. It, too, can be best introduced with reference to Aristotle. There is an open invitation in the *Ethics* to conceive of unjust exchange as a situation where one party's profit is the other party's loss, and of Aristotelian reciprocity or equivalence as eliminating such profits and losses by taking from one and giving to the other. Now if this is taken in terms of individual utilities, there is a suspicion of a gross misunderstanding of the nature of economics in this theoretical construction, and Aristotle and his followers have frequently been accused of harbouring it. Economic exchange is normally entered into in order to obtain an advantage in terms of utility, and normally *both parties profit* in these terms.

There is no question but that the scholastics understood this. If Aristotle is read more carefully, he says so himself. True equivalence, then, would mean that the exchanging parties *profit equally:* this would be the ideal realization of Aristotelian justice in exchange. But it involves interpersonal comparison of utilities, which we know to be a tricky affair. Fortunately, the common estimates of cost and market came to the rescue of the scholastic economists and took the problem out of the individual sphere. Another way to get around it is, of course, to leave exchangers to their own devices, each taking care of his own profit, which seems fair enough as long as there are effective checks to ensure that no party forgoes his advantage in absolute (rather than circumstantial) terms owing to fraud and coercion. This is also a relevant way to view the relationship between pricing *ad par* and pricing *ad pactum*.

But there is another side to it. If these checks have to be made operative, and a reasonable estimate has to replace a price reached by bargaining, it does not follow that a market estimate can always be substituted for a cost estimate. A minimum requirement would seem to be that each party at least *profits to some extent*. If the seller's actual cost or potential loss at parting with a commodity exceeds the normal competitive price, it is reasonable that he should be permitted to raise it to the level of his cost or potential loss – if the buyer is prepared to pay that much; otherwise the deal is off. This is extremely important for a proper grasp of the logic of scholastic usury doctrine, which applies this principle by analogy. It is a principle of *indemnity* which constitutes one half of what I like to call the scholastics' "double rule" of just pricing. The combination of the two halves of this rule (if not the elements themselves) seems to have originated with Thomas Aquinas in the *Summa theologiae*.[15] They came to be adopted by numerous later authors, including Olivi and Bernardino of Siena.

The other half of the double rule states that a price can*not* be driven up by the buyer's (rather than the seller's) utility, even if he is prepared to pay. Such preparedness to pay more than the just price is *prima facie* evidence of coercion. The seller in such an instance would be selling something which did not belong to him, said Aquinas. (We shall encounter this expression again in connection with usury teaching.) Olivi's answer to his second question cited above is therefore strictly negative: price cannot be based on buyer's utility. A surprising but quite consistent corollary to this conclusion is that the *nature* of the buyer's utility in a given situation is irrelevant. This is also a feature of scholastic economic reasoning essential for a proper understanding of usury doctrine. *Why* the buyer wants the commodity he buys is no business of the seller's. Corn for a starving household and corn to be resold at a profit should in

[15] II-II,77,1, p.276.

principle be treated in the same way: the seller can claim no share in the profit. The nature of the commodity in question ought not to make any difference either. Whether there is question of corn for the starving or truffles for a bishop's supper, the just price sets the limit. As mentioned above, the scholastics eventually began to distinguish between commodities, reserving their checks and correctives for necessaries and abandoning luxuries to the fortunes of free bargaining. I can find no similar distinction between different employments of a given commodity, which might be more relevant when comparing commodity exchange to money-lending. Anyhow, money was certainly a necessary to many medieval borrowers.

Two different types of cost estimates may thus serve to justify price in commodity exchange. On the one hand the seller may claim indemnity on the basis of actual cost. On the other hand normal cost may serve to indicate the just level of the market price where no such extraordinary claims intervene. The assumption that the competitive market price under normal conditions is a just price, which is now almost universally attributed to the scholastics, needs some qualifying remarks to clarify the relation between the market estimate and a cost estimate of the second type mentioned here. It ought to go without saying (though it seems sometimes to be overlooked) that the market price as a just norm always operates hypothetically only. If there is actually a competitive market in operation, there is no need for the moralist to preach justice in pricing, since the just price will establish itself anyhow. No buyer can be made to pay more (just as the seller can forget about his extraordinary costs). It is under monopoly and other market imperfections and particularly in isolated exchanges that undue pressure can be put on the buyer, thus calling for an estimate of *what the competitive price might have been.* A rough computation of normal cost may serve for this purpose, and this is all there is to the normal cost estimates of the scholastics. There is no reason to read into them any more specific anticipation of the kind of philosophical labour or cost theory of value which was subsequently to be encountered in classical and post-classical economists. Other types of just price estimates may serve equally well, such as those based on past experience and future guesses about markets, as well as on comparison with markets elsewhere in operation.

It is usual now to seek the basic justification of the competitive market price in scholastic economics in the fact that the market price provides a *common estimate* of value. This is a phrase frequently employed by the scholastics themselves. If we adopt it, we can say that reasonable common estimates made on other bases, (e.g. a cost basis) serve as substitutes for the real thing in the absence of such market conditions as can be relied upon to set the just price level automatically. The ultimate clue to scholastic economic ethics then lies in the word "common". What does it mean? Why is the common just? The terminology derives from the Roman law. "Common" as used in the present context evidently implies both the category of "usual" and the category of "joint". It may be difficult to distinguish clearly between these two categories, and their relative strengths changed subtly over time.

In the case of the generations of authors on which this study mainly focuses, I would suggest that emphasis be still placed on the "usualness" rather than the "jointness" of the common price estimates. The proposition that the competitive market price allocates joint social resources optimally is a later theoretical discovery and a later ethical premise. The scholastic economists of the thirteenth and fourteenth centuries set store by the common estimate less as a guideline to the common good than as a guarantee against exploitation made possible by singular circumstances. The fundamental proposition is that *the competitive market* to some extent *rules out duress*. Or, more precisely, it rules out the kind of duress that can justifiably be claimed. Common conditions offer as much protection against merely conditional consent as can well be expected of a system of justice in pricing. It is a primitive ethical idea, not foreign to Aristotle, that the usual is the natural and the natural is the just. The way God instituted society there will always be those who are too poor even to pay the normal market price. Such distress is the most bitter form of economic compulsion. It is a Christian duty to alleviate it by almsgiving. But that is a matter of charity not justice.

*

It is on the basis of this sketch of the principles underlying the scholastic analysis of justice in exchange of commodities that I would like to make a first approach to usury doctrine. Some points of similarity are immediately apparent. Thus both halves of the Thomist "double rule" of just pricing apply to usury by strict analogy. The seller's just claim to compensation for actual cost or potential loss exceeding a normal price estimate corresponds exactly to the so-called "extrinsic titles" to interest. The vulgar notion that the scholastics denied all interest in connection with money loans can be dismissed out of hand. In fact, *interesse* is a concept developed by them from Roman law. If the lender can show that parting with money will involve elements of cost or loss to him, he can justly demand indemnity for this from the borrower. The principle came to embrace both actual "emergent" loss (*damnum emergens*) and forgone "cessant" gain (*lucrum cessans*).

Conversely, the denial of the seller's right to profit from the buyer's utility finds its precise counterpart in the relationship between lender and borrower and accounts for the failure to discriminate between different classes of borrowers and different uses of borrowed money. Surprise has been voiced at this: why did not the scholastic moralists focus more on the "really" needy borrowers and let the rest fend for themselves? But according to the logic of Aristotelian justice, there is no way this distinction can be made. By the same token, there can be no difference in principle between loans for consumption and loans for investment. It is sometimes alleged that most loans in the Middle Ages were consumptive loans and that this fact explains (and even to some extent exonerates) the hatred of usury. On the literary evidence of the usury treatises, investment loans rather than consumptive loans are in the focus of theoretical attention. The two kinds may sometimes appear to be treated differently, but that would be on charitable grounds. From the point of view of justice, loan purpose is irrelevant.

For most of the century and more which has elapsed since Wilhelm Endemann contributed the first genuinely critical monograph to the history of scholastic economics, the points of similarity noted above could be explained easily as expressions of an underlying universal principle of justice embracing both commodity exchange and money-lending. In both areas of application, the first half of the double rule, assuring indemnity to seller or lender, can be interpreted as an extended cost principle. Similarly, the second half, denying profit on buyer's or borrower's utility, follows from the same cost principle, since such utility does not match any cost element. It was thus a general cost theory of value which lay at the heart of scholastic economics, according to this early modern interpretation. It held sway until late in the interwar period, when it began to look increasingly uncomfortable in the light of new research. It is now almost universally abandoned. The cost interpretation of the medieval just price doctrine, it is now alleged, was an ideological hang-up inviting selective reading of the sources. Cost hardly entered into it, according to some recent authors; the medieval just price was simply the competitive market price. I cannot personally subscribe to either the cost or the market interpretation of the just price as thus opposed to one another. In my opinion, the latter is as one-sided and as shakily based on selective reading of texts as was the former. Cost and market are really two sides to the doctrine, as I have tried to explain above.

In the wake of this historical reorientation, interpretation of scholastic usury doctrine has had to do without the pleasing analogy to just price doctrine which it used to enjoy. Writing in 1957, Noonan, subscribing wholeheartedly to the new market interpretation, sharply criticized previous attempts at unifying just price and usury theory. Such attempts can only lead to confusion, according to Noonan, for it is "one of the most striking features of scholastic economic thinking ... that the problem of the just price is treated from an entirely different viewpoint than that from which usury is considered".[16] The difference is not that the one is based on a market philosophy (which it is) while the other is based on a cost philosophy, but rather that the scholastics held a particular theory of money as an immutable value measure, while the values of other commodities were allowed to vary with demand according to the common estimation of men. I do not want to seem to differ more than is necessary with Noonan, whose grasp of the many facets of the usury problem as well as his grasp of sources (though he wrote too early to catch on to the compilatory character of Bernardino's work) makes his monograph still the best platform for future research in the area. I personally believe in the possibility of relating usury to just price doctrine, up to a point. Our disagreement turns on different interpretations of the Aristotelian theory of money, which is certainly fundamental to usury doctrine, but this, I think, can be resolved.

It is not uncommon for non-economists to confuse the value of money in the commodity market (i.e. the purchasing power of money in terms of commodities at a certain point of time) and the value of money in the money market (i.e. the value of having money at one's disposal for a certain period of time). As regards the former kind of value, it has been held by many modern critics that the scholastics identified the purchasing power of money with its legal face value which they held to be fixed and immutable. As far as the dominant Aristotelian school of monetary theory is concerned – the school which midway in the period between Olivi and Bernardino issued in Nicole Oresme's treatise on debasement – the literary evidence does not bear out this interpretation, as I have shown elsewhere.[17] As regards the second kind of value, however, it is true that the scholastics held some peculiar views as to its immutability. This is highly relevant to usury theory.

I suggest that the most fruitful approach to usury doctrine is to

[16] Noonan 82. For particulars regarding his position on this point, see Chapters IV and XX.

[17] Langholm (3).

maintain the analogy to just price doctrine as far as it goes and to take off from there. But it must be maintained on the basis of the whole structure as described in this chapter: the principle of indemnity prevailing, and the estimates of cost and market serving as checks and correctives to the bargaining process in order to prevent exploitation. The analogy is arrested by the proposition, held firmly by all the scholastics, that the use of money can have no positive market value. Thus one important variable of the system becomes a constant, and I gladly concede to the followers of Noonan that this makes the system look different, but its basic structure remains the same. No such thing as a competitive market for money, providing data for a market estimate, was available in the medieval economies, and the scholastics could think of no relevant general cost factors by which an alternative estimate could be made. So we can only assume, from what else they said, that if such a money market had existed, the scholastics would insist that its level must be identically zero. All payment for the use of money is therefore either indemnity under *extrinsic* titles, or otherwise the result of duress. Once this is established, all theory and all casuistry must focus on the nature and extent of extrinsic titles in order to separate just indemnity from unjust duress.

Why did the scholastics hold so firmly to the dogma that the use value of money, if permitted to establish itself freely, must be zero? A modern economic historian, looking back on the societies to which the scholastics addressed themselves, and knowing their ethical heritage, would most likely phrase his answer to this question differently than did the scholastics. To suggest a modern explanation is also part of our task, to which we shall return in our concluding chapter. What the scholastics themselves said, and that to which we shall devote the intervening four chapters making up the body of this book, is that the use of money cannot by the very nature of things, however men bargain with each other, have any value, money being by nature barren.

3. A teleology of money

Usury had been restricted by law or denounced by philosophers in all the Mediterranean societies from which Western Europe in the Middle Ages received its cultural heritage. Aristotle's practical philosophy was only translated in the complete texts from Greek into Latin around the middle of the thirteenth century: the *Ethics* a little before 1250, the *Politics* a little after. Long before that, the idea that usury is wrong because it forces a fruit from sterile money had travelled from the East through more devious channels. It arrived at the door of the early scholastics mainly by way of the writings of the Church Fathers. Thus, for instance, Gratian saw fit to include in the *Decretum* a fragment of St Basil's homily on Luke stating that usury makes gold breed gold,[1] and there are similar allusions in St Gregory of Nyssa[2] and in St Ambrose of Milan.[3] Although lines of transmission have long since become blurred, there is no reason to doubt that these various references give evidence of a common tradition, perhaps originating in Aristotle's *Politics*, perhaps only joined by Aristotle. For the present purpose of understanding the development of the scholastic theory, this question of origins is not of the first importance, nor shall we have to occupy ourselves much in this or subsequent chapters with the patristic tributary to the flow of tradition on this particular point.[4] Before the doctors of theology or canon law had had time to do much with the suggestions of the Fathers, the *Politics* appeared in Latin dress, and from then onwards the course of the tradition

[1] I,47,8; *Corpus Iuris Canonici*, ed. A. Friedberg, Leipzig 1879, I, 171.

[2] *Patrologia Graeca* (PG), ed. Migne, 44, 672; 46, 441.

[3] *Patrologia Latina* (PL), ed. Migne, 14, 774-7.

[4] But see below, pp.73-74 and note 6, with further reference to Chapter 5.

was entirely dominated by Aristotle's version of the sterility argument and by the particular context in which he stated it.

Aristotle's first mention of usury occurs in the *Nicomachean Ethics*. It is to be found in Book IV, which treats of a number of virtues somewhat related to wealth, starting with liberality. This virtue is in the nature of a mean between prodigality and meanness, says Aristotle, and as one example of the latter excess he mentions people engaged in certain degrading occupations, such as usurers, who "take from wrong sources, and more than their due".[5] This passage compresses into a minimum of space the author's precise attitude to wealth, expounded at greater length elsewhere. Wealth, to Aristotle, is a means not an end. To be wealthy consists rather in use than in possession, he says in the *Rhetoric*.[6] The principle is carried almost to the brink of absurdity. One of Aristotle's less convincing arguments in favour of private property, as listed in Book II of the *Politics*, is that one must own property in order to be able to distribute its fruits liberally to others.[7] Entirely despicable are those who focus on accumulation of wealth for its own sake, and particularly when this is done on a low scale, where men stoop to mean trades and dubious practices in order to convert two pieces of coin into three. The prototype of this is the petty usurer. The reference to him in the *Ethics* was mostly passed over lightly by the numerous textual expositors on that work, but some of those who commented in the form of questions took this opportunity to discuss a burning social issue of their times; it is here that one finds questions on usury by Odonis and Buridan. However, the locus remained greatly overshadowed by the much fuller discussion of monetary occupations and practices in the first book of the *Politics*.

Aristotle introduces the state by way of its component parts and spends several early chapters of the *Politics* on the subject of the household.[8] This calls for a distinction between two kinds

5 1121b; Rackham's translation; Loeb Classical Library, No. 73.

6 Book I, 1361b.

7 1263b.

8 On Aristotle's ideas about the nature of wealth and the use of money, see Langholm (3), Chapters 4 and 5.

of "wealth-getting", namely the necessary and laudable kind subservient to household management, and a perverse and despicable kind which seeks accumulation of wealth (or its attendant pleasures) as its final aim. Having explained the introduction of money, which particularly provides the means and the inspiration for this deplorable art of *chrematistics*, Aristotle a few pages further on reverts to the distinction (in one of the typical repetitions which mar some of his extant works) and in this connection mentions usury. William of Moerbeke's Latin translation of the *Politics*, which the scholastics used, is extremely literal, following the original closely as to syntax and sometimes copying the Greek words. I quote the section about usury in a somewhat freer modern English translation, inserting some of Moerbeke's key works in brackets.

> But, as we said, this art is twofold, one branch being of the nature of trade (*campsoria*) while the other belongs to the household art; and the latter branch is necessary and in good esteem, but the branch connected with exchange is justly discredited (for it is not in accordance with nature, but involves men's taking things from one another). As this is so, usury (*obolostatica*) is most reasonably hated, because its gain comes from money itself and not from that for the sake of which money was invented. For money was brought into existence for the purpose of exchange, but interest (*tokos*) increases the amount of money itself (and this is the actual origin of the Greek word: offspring resembling parent, and interest is money born of money); consequently this form of the business of getting wealth is of all forms the most contrary to nature.[9]

From the Latin version of this bit of text one may get the impression that the acceptable form of wealth-getting is to be contrasted to three perverse forms, described by the labels *campsoria, obolostatica*, and *tokos*. This tripartition was indicated in the commentary of Albert the Great and confirmed in that of Thomas Aquinas.[10] But it would seem, perhaps, that Aristotle had only a twofold distinction in mind here, and that the scholastic reading is due to Moerbeke's unsuccessful strug-

[9] 1258a-b; Rackham's translation; Loeb Class. Lib., No. 264.
[10] Albert, pp.60-1; Thomas, p.107.

gle with the Greek terms. To Aristotle, petty trade is despicable, for it takes money as its aim rather than the supply of necessaries for which it was invented, but worst of all forms of dealing in money is usury, which even discards all pretence at having to do with commodities and simply breeds money out of money directly. Thus while indirect exchange of commodities for money (as contrasted with barter of commodities for commodities) is under suspicion, money is in a sense a necessary evil, since it can also serve the good purpose of household management. But the prototype of its perverse employment is usury. This is probably the only distinction Aristotle had in mind and his sole reason for mentioning usury at all.

However, Moerbeke chose to render the Greek word meaning trade as *campsoria*, which meant that the kind of monetary activities which the scholastics on this authority must condemn did not per se include regular indirect exchange at all. Instead, it came to include money-changing, which is what was traditionally meant by *campsoria*, as well as two other kinds, where Aristotle at most intended only one. Moerbeke evidently capitulates completely here, in that he only renders the Greek words in Latin letters. *Obolostatica* is certainly petty usury; all modern translators render it thus. But the word means literally "weighing of coins", which is not precisely what the usurer does and can bring forth other associations. Thus Thomas Aquinas suggested that it could mean profiting *in excessu denariis instituendis*,[11] and this occasioned at least one fourteenth-century Thomist in this locus to condemn the practice of debasement of the currency.[12] Nicole Oresme, however, in his famous treatise against debasement associated *obolostatica* with *campsoria*.[13] No matter; we shall not be further concerned with this particular perverse form of money-making. When usury appears in the scholastic catalogue at all, it is because of the word *tokos*, which the early commentators understood to mean

[11] Loc.cit.

[12] Vernani, f.66ra.

[13] *De moneta*, ed. Johnson, London 1956, p.27. On the Aristotelian bases of Oresme, see Langholm (3), *passim*.

usury. This is indicated in Albert the Great's commentary, and Aquinas provides the definition: *tokos, id est usura.*[14] Now *tokos* in Greek means offspring, as well as usury, thus suggesting a powerful simile: usury is that form of wealth-getting which makes money breed money, which is against nature because only natural organisms can breed.

This is the notorious Aristotelian theory of the sterility of money. While it rests partly on a word, the classical scholar will warn us multilingual moderns of the awful *reality* of words in ancient Greece. The barbarian tongues spoke nonsense: Greek was the vehicle of truth, in which word and thing could easily become one.[15] To Aristotle, therefore, usury as offspring was presumably something more than a pun. To us it can be only that, and to make it serve as a basis of social policy must seem absurd. It is as though all Aristotle had to say about this particular kind of monetary activity is that since usury means offspring, and since money is an artificial thing which cannot generate any offspring, therefore usury is unnatural and therefore it is wrong. Stated like that, the doctrine fell easy prey to the ridicule of post-scholastic economists. Many must have been those who enjoyed Bentham's picture of Aristotle (the first great zoologist) frantically turning pieces of coin over in search of organs of generation and, finding none, solemnly proclaiming money to be sterile.[16]

That this is unfair to Aristotle is beyond doubt, but it is also beyond our immediate concern here, just as the primary object of Bentham's attack was medieval not classical prejudice. Is it fair criticism of the scholastics? Did they really read Aristotle like this and take him at face value? It is often difficult to say on the basis of the texts they have left us. The commentators on the *Politics* would sometimes only paraphrase Aristotle, and then they may certainly sound as though they are making biological

[14] Loc.cit.

[15] Barker 385-6.

[16] *Defence of Usury*, Letter X ("Grounds of the Prejudices against Usury"); in *Jeremy Bentham's Economic Writings*, ed. W.Stark, Vol.I, London 1952, p.158.

observations: "Usury treats of money as though it were a natural thing capable of reproducing itself in kind",[17] "but to reproduce itself is only conceded to natural things not to artefacts".[18] Outside the ranks of commentators, the clinching example must be Giles of Rome in his exceedingly influential *De regimine principum:*

> Animals, because they are natural things, generate their equals, and give birth and increase themselves. But he who desires that coins (*denarii*) multiply themselves, so that ten after a lapse of time become twenty, desires that artefacts multiply themselves, and since this is against the nature of artefacts, a *denarius* being something artificial, that is well said which is said in the first book of the *Politics*, that usury is abominable and against nature.[19]

Now Giles of Rome also kept quite close to Aristotle's texts; his arguments are often paraphrases. Moreover, in the preceding chapter he had already argued about the unnaturalness of usury along a different line (as we shall see presently). He does not really need the zoological simile, but it must have seemed irresistible. Further removed from the text of the *Politics* we mostly find paler references to it: "Money does not of its *nature* have any fruit" (Scotus[20]); "it is against *nature* that money should breed money" (Gerson[21]). It is difficult to know what to make of this. Only the contexts can explain it.

However, to the extent that the scholastics did take Aristotle's simile in earnest (as some of them must surely have done), or even to the extent that they found it worthwhile using as a mere simile (as perhaps Giles did), there is something else which they shared with and even inherited from Aristotle to at least partly excuse it – an excuse we can no longer claim. It is not that they were unilingual in the sense explained above. They were in fact in better command of languages than many modern economists are: Latin was (at best) the second language to every one of them;

[17] Burley, f.206ra.
[18] (Pseudo?)-Trevet, f.5vb.
[19] II,iii,11, ff.221v-222r.
[20] *Sent.*IV,15,2, p.293.
[21] Col.172.

besides, the pun is not even in Latin. But while they could thus easily see through the word to the thing as far as *tokos* is concerned, when it came to money, they had difficulties looking through the concrete object to the abstract concept. Giles of Rome states the argument quoted above in terms of the penny (*denarius*), a coin, not in terms of money in general, and that is highly significant.

Money in the abstract, as a claim, a right, a power, is not an Aristotelian but a legal idea. It came to scholastic thought from Roman law partly through canon law and eventually contributed strongly to the overthrow of its usury theory, sterility and all. To Aristotle, money is a physical object. Having explained why it came to be invented, he proceeds to describe its required physical properties: it must be made of metal, be portable, easy to handle, with a stamp of the amount impressed on it.[22] Whenever Aristotle speaks of money he speaks of *coin*. In the thirteenth century this was something that would still be absorbed without reflection; it confirmed a primitive idea still current. I would suggest that this is perhaps the single most important thing to realize in order to grasp the Aristotelian theory of usury: it was a theory based on the conception of money as coin. It is such a fateful idea – most modern economists would probably say: such a potentially misleading idea. It is this idea mostly that gives force to the biological simile. Money is an artefact only, shaped from metal, so obviously dead and fruitless. If you will lend it, says Antonio to Shylock, lend it to your enemy and not as to your friends, "for when did friendship take a breed for barren metal of his friend?"[23]

Poetic imagery aside, however, the fact that money is a lifeless coin cannot carry much conviction as an argument against usury, because it is not consistent with other rulings as to what constituted usury and what was legitimate gain. To anticipate briefly our succeeding chapter, it was accepted from Roman law that usury could be committed in all fungibles and that it was limited to a particular kind of contract which did not include a

[22] 1257a.

[23] Shakespeare, *The Merchant of Venice*, Act.I,3.

lease. But a lifeless thing could be leased for profit. It is useful to record this counter-argument from the pen of Gerardo of Siena, since he was one of those who contributed most to the building of a consistent theory:

> Another argument is also commonly employed (against usury), which seems to derive from the Philosopher in *Politics*, I. Its basis consists in this: that it is against nature that artificial things should breed and generate and thus multiply. But in a usurious contract, coin (*denarius*), which is artificial, breeds coin and multiplies in the aforesaid way. Therefore, by the nature of the thing, this kind of contract is unnatural and consequently vicious. Yet neither does this argument seem to be valid, for two reasons. First, because usury is committed not only in artificial things but also in natural things, for instance in wine, oil, or the like, and therefore the argument does not apply to them. Second, because a house can be seen to be an artificial thing, and yet within a certain period of time someone might profit from a house as much as another house is worth, and thus a house would give birth to a house.[24]

So much for the inability of artificial things to breed. If the sterility of money is to be maintained as a rational argument against usury, it must be put on a different basis from the biological one. Now Gerardo of Siena, for one, did so maintain it, and in the writings of those who followed him it played a double role. It was partly stated as an analytical premise in its own right, and in that sense its restatement and adjustment are largely due to Gerardo in a tradition from Thomas Aquinas through Peter Olivi. But in addition many later scholastics continued the practice of the earlier ones of using it less seriously as a punchline to round off a *finalistic* argument as to why usury is wrong. Sometimes these arguments become confused; it is difficult to say what is premise and what is conclusion – just as it is in Aristotle's own words as quoted. Nevertheless, the relationship between the two lines of thinking is important, for when the Latin scholastics had to withdraw from Aristotle's uncompromising teleology, they fell back on the sterility of money (on its new foundation) in order to defend the

24 P.176.

compromise. How they came to conceive of sterility in a new way, is the subject of our next three chapters. What remains to be explained within the context of Aristotle is why they needed it.

When Aristotle takes up the question of the social function of money in the *Politics*, what weighs on him is the danger of a perversion of the *purpose* for which it was invented. Money, like all things Greek, has a *telos*. It is man-made, but it is made to serve a natural end. However, it can also be misused for perverse, man-made ends. Aristotle must take some of the blame for our fondness of that ambiguous word, "natural". When the scholastics read him to say that it is unnatural for money to breed money, they probably misunderstood Aristotle. I think most scholars now agree that his real point is not that usury is an unnatural use of money because money *cannot* breed (which is what the usurer tries to make it do); rather his point is that money *should not* be made to breed (a simile of what it does in usury) because usury is an unnatural use of money. What this would indicate is that Aristotle in fact recognized the productivity of money. He did not think money sterile at all, he just hated its fruits. Some scholars have read him like that.[25] The question slips away into the mysteries of Greek philology. In the case of those who were obliged to read Aristotle through Moerbeke, the tendency was to take the finalistic proposition and the sterility proposition as mutually supporting. In scholastic writing it is therefore sometimes difficult to decide in which direction the argument is meant to flow. Aristotle may even seem to contradict himself. An illustration of this, as well as a firm point of departure for a discussion of the finalistic argument, is provided by Nicole Oresme's résumé of Aristotle on usury in his treatise against debasement:

[25] Cf., for example, Cannan 106. The "symposium" to which Cannan contributed this opinion also contains interesting reflections by other scholars (see Bibliography). A decade later, M.Defourny (15) in a penetrating study of the *Politics* confirmed the suggestion that Aristotle probably held money to be productive rather than sterile. This may also be implied in Newman's (II, 196) explanation of the text in his classical study of the work.

But it is monstrous and unnatural that an unfruitful thing should bear, that a thing specifically sterile, such as money, should bear fruit and multiply of itself. Therefore when profit is made from money, not by laying it out in the purchase of natural wealth, its proper and natural use, but by changing it into itself, as changing one form of it for another, or giving one form for another, such profit is vile and unnatural. It is by this reasoning that Aristotle proves, in the first book of the *Politics*, that usury is against nature, because the natural use of money is as an instrument for the exchange of natural wealth, as has frequently been said. Anyone therefore who uses it otherwise, misuses it against the natural institution of money, for he causes money to beget money, which, as Aristotle says, is against nature.[26]

While Oresme begins here by stating that money is sterile and ends up by suggesting that it is not, he is not to be misunderstood as to what the purpose of money is; it is to be "laid out in the purchase of natural wealth". The word *instrumentum* as used in the Latin original, as well as other ambiguous words occurring in the Aristotelian texts, such as *medium* and even *mensura*, have led some critics to find in Aristotle a confirmation of an earlier medieval conception of money, rooted in the feudal, largely barter-orientated economy, according to which its main function is to serve as a measure of value. I must warn against this misconception. Attempts to explain scholastic usury theory on such a basis must fail. That theory, in so far as it was Aristotelian, as I said above, was based on money in the concrete. This means not only that the conception of money as an abstract claim was foreign to it, but also that money as an abstract measure was at best secondary to it. It was influenced by a focus on the function which money in the concrete is first and foremost designed to serve, namely to be a *means of exchange*.

If it is to be called an instrument, it is primarily so in Oresme's sense of an instrument to get exchange going rather than a measuring instrument. If it is a medium, it is so in the sense of a means or an intermediary in exchange rather than in the sense of a measure. "Money, as the Philosopher says", explains Alex-

[26] Johnson's translation, ed.cit., pp. 25-26.

ander Lombard, "was invented in order to be an intermediary between seller and buyer (*medium inter vendentem et ementem*) for the exchange of the necessaries of life".[27] As a summary of Aristotle's position, this is correct in the simplest and most direct sense imaginable. Coins are struck in order to pass from hand to hand in lieu of goods when direct barter is inconvenient. Money is to rest briefly in any hand only in the expectation of suitable purchases; it is thus a "surety" (as Aristotle says in the *Ethics*[28]) for someone who has given up his own good and still awaits its exchange for another suitable good. Now this waiting introduces a time element and the possibility of sifting off sums of money to be lent and increased: money as a *store of wealth* is what poses the problem of usury. But it is a secondary function. Money as a *measure of value* is also secondary. When money and goods change hands, the requirement of equivalence implies measurement, but a coin is normally a measure only because it intervenes in the physical exchange.[29]

In regular exchange money is intermediary not only between seller and buyer; in a more visual sense it is intermediary between thing sold and thing bought. The formula made famous by Marx is latent in this first book of the *Politics:* C-M-C (Commodity-Money-Commodity).[30] Money appears between extremes or termina in the form of commodities. In money-changing and usury money is itself terminus: M-M. This is against the purpose for which it was invented. Henry of Ghent: "Money is *medium* in exchange and not *terminus*".[31] Alexander Lombard: "Money should not be able to be bought and sold, for it is not *extremum* in selling or buying but *medium*".[32]

But the *telos* of a thing does not sound like a very convincing

[27] Ed. Hamelin, p.126; cf. p.165.

[28] 1133b.

[29] For a fuller documentation of the views expressed in this paragraph, see Langholm (3), particularly Chapter 6.

[30] Actually W-G-W (Ware-Geld-Ware); cf. *Das Kapital, Werke*, Vol.23, Berlin 1962, p.162ff.

[31] *Quodl.*VI,22, f.242r.

[32] P.165.

moral criterion. Granted that money was invented in order to be used in one way, why should it be wrong to use it in another way? What is there in the natural law to say that a thing must always be used for one specific purpose only, asked Summenhart, criticizing the finalistic argument. It would mean that it is sinful, for instance, to place money in a shoe, since that is to use the shoe for a purpose for which it was not ordained.[33] Now this is not fair criticism of Aristotle, and the example of the shoe is singularly maladroit in his case, since Aristotle himself had taken the shoe as an example to show that a thing *has* more than one use: A shoe is made to be worn, but it can also be exchanged for other things ("money or food").[34] Aristotle does not condemn the transition from self-sufficiency to a barter economy, which brings with it such secondary uses of things – (which turns things into "commodities" in the first place). Perhaps Summenhart wants to demonstrate internal inconsistency in Aristotle. In that case, he misses the underlying point. It is revealed in the continuation of our quotation from Henry of Ghent above: "To make the exchange medium a terminus *for greater profit*, is usury".

The *telos* of things is subordinated to the *telos* of man. A thing is used wrongly if it leads the user astray. For Aristotle to strive after wealth for its own sake is to mistake means for end. A modicum of material wealth is a necessary condition for the good life of man and household. The household may produce a surplus of one useful object which cannot readily be bartered for another useful object of which the household is short, but money may serve as a medium to bring about exchange between them. In this function money serves the ulterior purpose of the household. But even regular commodity exchange can misuse money if its purpose is accumulation. Marx's formula is part of a continuous chain: C-M-C-M-. What is terminus depends on the motivational focus. In household management, the focus is on the supply of necessaries. The petty trader focuses on money: he buys in order to sell again at a profit. In this sense money is

[33] Q.23, ad 8, p.90.
[34] 1257a.

terminus to him; his operations start and end with money on hand: M-C-M. More and more money for each link in the chain, Aristotle insinuates. Why else should he engage in this type of activity?

In the formula applying to money-changing and usury, there is no commodity element present at all, and thus, as Aristotle is bound to see it, no possible connection with an ulterior redeeming purpose. All there is is money; it is beginning and end: M-M. The sole purpose of such exchanges must be to make these termina unequal and thus bring forth an unjust fruit. The only possible motive is greed for money. The early textual commentators on the *Politics* took this point immediately. *Avarice*, according to Albert the Great, is what motivated other uses of money, for instance usury, by which money is made to breed money.[35] Or in a longer quotation to vindicate Giles of Rome, whose somewhat naïve version of the sterility argument was reproduced above:

> The other three kinds (of monetary transactions) are justly blamed, for any art which begins with money and ends with money, would seem to place its end in money. *Campsoria*, therefore, *obolostatica*, and *usura*, since they exist almost entirely in money, because they begin with money and end with money, are blameworthy according to the Philosopher; for that man seems to be too greedy for money (*nimis enim videtur esse denariorum cupidus*) whose actions begin with money and end with money.[36]

However, the Latin scholastics soon were in retreat from Aristotle's rigid positions. Recognition of the social usefulness of indirect exchange by means of money was a victory already won in opposition to patristic prejudice. The flourishing of towns and markets had legitimized the merchants' profession: men who engaged in chains of exchanges and lived on the monetary gains. There was nothing the moralist could do about that except admonish the merchant to respect the just price and cost estimates, including risk and a decent support of himself

[35] P.61; cf. also, for instance, Giles of Lessines, p.416.
[36] Op.cit., II,iii,10, f.221r.

and his family, and to distribute the happy windfall among the poor: in short, not to set his sights on money as such but to live by Aristotelian and Christian ideals. Aristotle could not have imagined such an "Aristotelian" merchant. Fortunately, the scholastics received a Latin *Politics* where the condemnation of trade had disappeared, since the word for trade was rendered by Moerbeke as *campsoria*, meaning money-changing.

Next, *campsoria* (if not *obolostatica*, whose meaning the scholastics could not quite agree about) came to be legitimized as well, though with evident reluctance and caution by those who set most store by Aristotelian doctrine. Trade provided a precedent. By analogy, it was conceded that those who supplied merchants and others with appropriate coins and currencies performed a useful service. While money was not invented in order to be bought and sold, it was necessary, so that exchange of commodities might flow smoothly between regions, to have somebody engage in this type of activity. But note: it had to be conducted in good faith, not for enrichment and out of love of money, but only for the support of the *campsor* and his dependants, in the form of a reasonable charge for "counting and guarding money and other things which pertain to its care". Otherwise, says Henry of Ghent, concluding a question about money-changing in one of his *quodlibeta*, "it is in no way permitted but is a species of usury, which the Philosopher calls *tokos*, and of which he says that it reproduces itself".[37]

But why draw the line there? Why not extend the analogy from changing money to lending money? Both are equally useful and necessary banking services. If the *campsor* can take a dividend to support himself and his dependants, why not the *usurarius*? In his treatise on economic contracts Gerald Odonis criticizes Olivi's seven natural law arguments against usury. The seventh argument is the "*telos cum tokos*" argument from Aristotle according to which generating money by money is an unnatural use.[38] In reply to this, Odonis subtly shifts the emphasis from use to user and suggests a differentiation according

[37] Quaest.cit., f.243r.
[38] Olivi, f.302ra.

to motive. To seek endless accumulation of money is condemned because it implies the impoverishment of others (a sentiment never expressed by Aristotle), but not "to seek moderately to maintain one's own indemnity in lending it".[39] This is probably as close to allowing "moderate usury" as it is possible to come in an early Aristotelian author.

However, while the tendency in all of Odonis' replies to Olivi is to favour the claims of the creditor, there is nothing in what he says which cannot reasonably be construed as justifying *extrinsic* titles. Read like that, he is in accord with subsequent scholastic development, where the basically non-Aristotelian modification already applied to trade and to money-changing for profit may well be said to have been extended to lending at *interest.* But nowhere does Odonis or his followers place *tokos* in a class with *campsoria.* I would suggest that there is probably nothing in the Aristotelian text that could have saved this barrier from collapse had that text happened upon a doctrinal milieu less firmly entrenched in its opposition to usury than was Europe in the thirteenth century. In the circumstances, conceding extrinsic titles, the scholastics maintained the distinction. The services of the money-changer, like those of the merchant, are subject to a just value estimate. The services of the money-lender can be subject to no such estimate. They are worth nil. Why? In the final analysis, for no other reason than that money is sterile. If the question of a redeeming motivation is raised, it must be parried in the same way. This position is clearly stated in Gerardo of Siena's version of the finalistic argument, with which we may suitably close this chapter. In addition to its primary use, says Gerardo by way of introduction, a thing may without blame be applied to secondary uses out of necessity but not out of cupidity:

> One may use money in exchange for life's necessaries, and this is its proper use for which it was invented. One may also use it in exchange for other currencies which are encountered where one lives or travels, and this is its secondary use which is appropriately permitted since

[39] Odonis, f.92r.

just equality can be observed. But he acts viciously who uses money for lending with the intention of receiving something above the principal, such as does the usurer, who misuses it by making money breed money, of which it is not capable, nor is this its proper use. And this seems to be the intention of Aristotle in the first book of the *Politics*, where he calls usury the fruit of money; for which reason he also says that it is most unnatural; for it is certainly neither by nature nor by art that money manages to have this use and this fruit, but by downright human malice and cupidity.[40]

The finalistic argument does not hold unless an honourable motive can be absolutely ruled out in the case of usury. To manage this, Gerardo falls back on sterility. But a few pages back the same author repudiated the sterility argument in its crude form where it states that artefacts cannot breed.[41] If sterility is to be a mere simile to round off the finalistic argument (as many scholastics evidently used it), Gerardo's version of it is circular. It can thus be a valid argument only if the sterility of money is understood to mean something altogether different, and if this different meaning embodies a true economic proposition. Gerardo of Siena contributed, along with others, to such a redefinition of the sterility concept. It was an analytical tradition which originated far back in patristic sources and proceeded via a number of other natural law arguments against usury.

[40] P.182.

[41] See above, p.61.

4. The legal framework

In his critical history of interest theories, the nineteenth-century Austrian economist Eugen von Böhm-Bawerk summarized the teaching of the medieval canonists on usury in four points. According to these authors, "the lender is paid in interest for fruits which barren money cannot bear. He sells a "use" which does not exist, or a use which already belongs to the borrower. And finally, he sells time, which belongs to the borrower just as much as it does to the lender and to all men".[1] There is presumably more than one way to break down the body of teaching to which Böhm-Bawerk refers here. However, if one considers the twelve arguments against usury listed by Bernardino of Siena in his thirty-eighth sermon or even the double number lined up for attack by Conrad Summenhart, one will find that most of them can be arranged under one or another of those four headings. In fact Molinaeus, through whose treatise Summenhart's criticism reached a larger circle of readers, made the same selection of three main arguments for closer examination, omitting only the argument that time is non-vendible, which he did not deign to take seriously.[2]

Böhm-Bawerk did not let himself be caught in that error. Being one of the originators of the modern time-orientated explanation of interest in his own positive theory soon to follow the critical history, he would be bound to pay attention to what

[1] Böhm-Bawerk I, 25. I quote the English version by W.Smart (*Capital and Interest*, London 1890) at p.23.

[2] Molinaeus, p.537. These three scholastic arguments are also the ones explicitly countered by Turgot, writing midway in time between Molinaeus and Böhm-Bawerk. Cf. *Mémoire sur les prêts d'argent,* in *Oeuvres*, ed. E.Daire, Vol.1, Paris 1844, pp.103-154 at pp.122-130.

the scholastic economists said about the time factor. It is true that they soon grew suspicious of the time argument themselves in its original form, but it persisted in the undercurrent of their tradition throughout. We shall return to the early time argument in connection with a systematic discussion of money and time in Chapter 6. Since this study focuses on the Aristotelian elements of usury theory, we shall be concerned in every chapter with the first item in Böhm-Bawerk's list, stating the proposition that money is barren. The more precise purpose of the present chapter, then, is to look into the body of usury doctrine from the points of view of the two middle items in the list, which argue against usury in terms of the existence and ownership of the use value of money.

While Böhm-Bawerk probably took the designation "canonist" in a wider sense than I am inclined to do here and might even have included both Bernardino of Siena and Summenhart within their later ranks, the arguments to which he refers can be called canonistic arguments in a narrower sense as well. Each of them can be traced back, directly or indirectly, to an origin in Church legislation.

As a statement of the orthodox social ethics of the Middle Ages, no single body of textual evidence surpasses in importance the collection of canons originally compiled by the monk Gratian towards the end of the twelfth century and known to the scholastics as the *Decretum*. An early addition to this compilation (a so-called *palea*) contains in more or less embryonic form a number of the central arguments against usury based on natural reason and subsequently developed by the scholastics. It is a bit of text referred to as *Eiciens* (from its incipit). Much older than Gratian, it dates perhaps from the fifth or sixth century and is extracted from a homily on Matthew, commenting on the passage where Christ threw the merchants out of the Temple.[3] The scholastic users of this text attributed it falsely to St John Chrysostom. The anonymous author gathers his objections to usury together in this remarkable passage:

[3] Matthew 21, 12-13.

More cursed than all merchants is the usurer, for he sells a thing not bought, as do the merchants, but given by God, and afterwards takes back his good, removing that of another with his own; a merchant, however, does not take back a good once sold. Yet someone says: is not he who lends a field in order to receive produce or a house in order to receive rent, similar to him who lends money at usury? Far from it. First, because money is put out for no use except to buy things; second, because one who has a field may get a fruit from it by cultivation, one who has a house gets from it the use of habitation. Therefore the lender of a field or a house is seen to give up his own use and receive money and in a way, as it were, to exchange gain for gain; from money laid up you get no benefit. Third, a field or a house deteriorates in use; but money, when lent, neither diminishes nor deteriorates.[4]

The "thing not bought but given by God" which the usurer is accused of selling, was taken by the early canonists to mean time, and so this place in the law supplied authority for some heavy preaching and some more hesitant reasoning about the sin of selling God's time. The suggestion that the usurer takes back something truly belonging to the borrower could be taken in two ways or at least taken with different emphases. The emphasis could be economic, suggesting that what the borrower is made to pay back beyond the principal is the fruit of his own *industry*. Taken in this sense it becomes a particular variant of the argument from sterility and this variant will be discussed fully in the chapter to follow. Alternatively, the emphasis could be legal, referring to the particular form of contract to which usury was limited according to the scholastic definition. In this version a broad tradition took off from *Eiciens*, and we shall return to it presently.

At this point in the text the anonymous author reports on a question posed in opposition to the condemnation of usury, and rounds off by making a reply in three points. This question was destined to be asked rhetorically again and again throughout the scholastic tradition and even later, since it was much favoured also by those intent on proving that the replies of pseudo-

[4] *Decretum*,I,88,11; ed. Friedberg, 309. A Latin version of pseudo-Chrysostom is in PG 56, 840. This is most likely a rather free translation of a Greek original, now lost; cf. Bardenhewer III, 597.

Chrysostom and all additions made to these replies, are really inadequate to meet the objection. This, then, became the key general "case" of the scholastic usury debate: How is it that a field or a house (a horse is often added later as a third example) can be lent at a profit while money must be lent for free?

In the first two replies proffered by the author behind *Eiciens* one immediately recognizes Aristotle in the finalistic argument and in the sterility argument. As in the case of some occurrences reported on at the opening of the preceding chapter,[5] there can be no doubt that we have here another outlet of the same Greek tradition. This means that the scholastic economists actually encountered the Aristotelian approach to usury half a century or more before the *Politics* became available. However, like some less important lines of this tradition, the lines passing through canon law on the whole mingled with and were soon swallowed up by the broader one from the *Politics*. If they could do so to the extent which they evidently did, this is not least due to some surprising and most fortunate work of editing the ancient text. There are in fact some peculiarities of transmission of both the Aristotelian arguments as they came to be adapted from pseudo-Chrysostom.

In *Eiciens* as quoted, money was made "to buy things" (*ad emendum*). This is money's *telos* as understood by Aristotle. But in the ancient original which the *palea* paraphrases, the line reads, *ad pretium emendi vel vendendi*. According to this version, money was made not to be a means of exchange but to be a measure of value. This is definitely non-Aristotelian (at least so in the context of the *Politics*). It takes us back to a conception of money's role which some historians have associated with early medieval economics. The rewriting in *Eiciens* which suited the advent of Aristotle so well, may of course have been largely accidental, but it could also be taken as a sign of the ripening of ideas which made the acceptance of Aristotle so natural and easy. Passing on to the second reply made by pseudo-Chrysostom to the question comparing money-lending to the lending of other kinds of property, namely that fields

[5] See above, p.54 with notes 1 to 3.

yield fruits and houses yield use-value while money does not, one finds by comparing the texts that a degree of rewriting has been done here as well. By this process, some un-Aristotelian associations were made to flow less freely from this locus, and *Eiciens* could be used as a welcome confirmation of what was read about the sterility of money in the *Politics*. However, these associations were not entirely strangled. Moreover, the Latin version of pseudo-Chrysostom was also known directly. This caused a certain amount of embarrassment when some of the late scholastics, finding the biological sterility argument to be a failure, tried to prove sterility from *Eiciens*. This episode is best explained within the context of the fruitfulness of human industry, and I beg to postpone it to the next chapter.[6]

This takes us to the bottom of the list of arguments against usury in *Eiciens*, and to the third reply to the question posed in opposition, namely that money, unlike other objects legitimately lent at a profit, does not deteriorate in use. This was one canon law argument which met with little favour even among the relatively early scholastics. Still upheld by the Franciscans Alexander of Hales (or rather by the compilers of the *Summa theologica* bearing his name) and Bonaventura,[7] it was rejected before the end of the thirteenth century by the Dominican theologians, Albert the Great and Thomas Aquinas, on the ground that it lacks general validity. Not all non-monetary objects deteriorate in use (for instance, says Aquinas, a house need not do so); still they may be lent at a profit.[8] In fact, as the scholastics came to agree, so may money itself when lent for non-monetary (for instance, display) purposes. Then it remains intact and a charge for its use is not usury.[9]

[6] See below, p.106.

[7] Alexander of Hales, *Summa*,III, p.567; Bonaventura, *Sent.*III,37, p.836.

[8] Albert, *Sent.*III,37,13, p.708; Thomas, *Sent.*III,37,1,6, pp.429-430; cf. *De malo*,XIII,4, p.375. Cf. also, for instance, Giles of Rome, *Quodl.*V,24, f.75va.

[9] That it must logically be permitted to lend money at a profit provided that ownership remains with the lender, was pointed out by William of Auxerre (*Summa*,III,21, f.223rb), one of the first theologians to use the ownership argument. Such contracts of money for display or similar purposes were to become something of an embarrassment to the late scholastics as well; see folowing chapter, p.107.

According to the principle which can be seen to emerge here, the significant distinction between lending money and lending (or rather leasing) a horse or a house (or money for non-monetary purposes), turns on the question of ownership. It is a legal distinction, and the scholastics soon shifted its foundation from canon law to Roman law. The ancient jurists had compiled a list of different, very precisely defined economic contracts, some of them referring to loans. It is this legal tradition which speaks already in William of Auxerre (and in Alexander of Hales copying William) when he counters this kind of objection to usury doctrine by explaining that two different kinds of contract are involved in the two cases.[10] To lend a horse (or a house or a golden vessel) is a *locatio*, a contract where ownership does not pass to the borrower. It is therefore just that the owner of the horse receive payment for the use of his property. But lending money for its normal purpose is a contract of *mutuum*, where ownership passes, the money becoming the property of the borrower, and it is therefore unreasonable and unjust that the lender should reap a profit from someone else's property. The contract of *mutuum* is restricted to fungibles, where repayment can be made not in the very objects lent but in equivalent objects of the same species; it is not restricted to money but can be concluded in commodity fungibles as well. This kind of contract, according to the *Digest*,[11] consists in those things which are given by weight, number and measure, such as wine, oil, corn or money – to be paid back in the same kind and quantity.

One of the things which makes a horse different from a house is that one is a "natural" living creature while the other is an "artificial" dead object. If one tends to deteriorate in use while the other does not, this is irrelevant to usury, since both are non-fungibles. The justification of usury doctrine must be established on other bases. Linking up with our preceding chapter, we are now in a position to examine Gerardo of Siena's rejection

[10] William, loc.cit.; Alexander, pp.565-7, 911-3.
[11] 12,1,2,1.

of the biological sterility argument from Aristotle in the same light.[12] As will be found by glancing back and comparing with the table below, Gerardo makes two comparisons.

Objects	Fungible	Non-fungible
Artificial	Money	House
Natural	Wine	Horse

"Artefacts cannot breed" - proposition rejected

Contracts of *mutuum* Sterility to be shown

One is horizontal in the table, within the class of artefacts. A house is an artefact, but when it is leased, it can be said to breed another house. Hence some artefacts can indeed breed – or rather, some artefacts can be allowed to breed. In the case of the house, this is not usury, since the lease of the house is a *locatio*. The other comparison is vertical in the table, within the class of fungibles. The question whether artefacts can or cannot breed is also irrelevant because usury is not limited to artefacts. Lending wine at a profit is hit by the usury prohibition, but wine is a natural fungible. (The condition of its being usury is that the contract is a *mutuum*, but this would be the normal condition in the case of wine as well, perhaps more so than in the case of money: who would borrow wine except for the purpose of drinking it or reselling it?) If the sterility proposition is to have any force in this *schema* it must be shown to be valid not for all artefacts but for all fungibles.

In all the scholastic texts to be examined in the sequel, usury must be understood to be limited to contracts of *mutuum*. This

[12] See above, p.61.

was not originally the case, and in popular preaching the word lived on, bearing a wider connotation reminiscent of the exhortations of some of the Church Fathers who spoke freely of usury in connection with almost any kind of oppressive business deal. The sharpened definition is due to the late twelfth- and early thirteenth-century commentators and summarists on the canon law, who adopted the Roman law definitions of contracts. Restricting usury to contracts of *mutuum* does not imply a general loosening of the reins on other types of contract. Nevertheless, it made a certain difference whether a transgression was to be classified as usury or merely as some other less heinous type of sin. Hence the endless casuistry seeking to determine when some elaborate arrangement involving delayed payment included an element of *mutuum* and therefore of usury and when it was all a sales contract where the most that could be criticized was an unjust price. It may be worth noting (though it shifts the burden of historical interpretation away from the kind of intellectual factors on which this study focuses) that this strict formal limitation to a particular kind of loan contract, to the extent that it takes the pressure off other types, tends to favour those contracts which may seem to have been more immediately beneficial to societies emerging from feudal conditions. A modern society is commercial before it is capitalistic; it needs professional merchants before it needs money-lenders. The one profession soon needs the other, but there was a period when moralists could reasonably distinguish between them and it more or less coincides with the period examined here.

The defining of usury in such a way that it can be argued against on the basis of the transfer of ownership was naturally welcome to the polemicist. When money borrowed is actually the property of the borrower, he must be allowed to use it as he sees fit in the period stipulated without any claim arising on the part of the lender to receive part or all of the profit reaped by the borrower. The lender can only hope to get back an equal amount (or weight or number or measure) of the fungible in question; that is all he gave and all he can legitimately take back. Usury, viz. any repayment above this principal, according to this argument, becomes a kind of theft, since it consists in taking what belongs to another. It is no coincidence that the scholastics in their numerous commentaries on the *Sentences* of Peter Lombard found one suitable place to discuss usury in Distinction 37 of Book III, which deals with theft in connection with the Commandments. (The other standard locus of usury doctrine in the *Sentences* is to be found in connection with restitution for sinful economic gain in Book IV.) If the legal technicality is accepted (and who is the repentant merchant to discuss law with the doctors), the force of this argument must have been tremendous. When Molinaeus criticized it in the sixteenth century, he attributed it to John Duns Scotus, third in the line of prominent Franciscan authorities. It was Scotus (actually taking over the argument from Alexander of Hales and Bonaventura), who coined the phrase, often repeated, that the usurer "sells what is not his own".[13] Other exponents of the principle include familiar names like Peter Olivi and Alexander Lombard.[14]

One reason why ownership was considered to be important is that *risk* normally follows ownership. In one of the places where Alexander of Hales asks why money may not be lent at a profit while it is permitted to lease a house, a horse, or a golden vessel, he gives the four reasons: viz. that ownership passes, that risk passes, that money does not deteriorate, and that it is barren.[15] In the casuistry of the scholastics, risk became an important criterion. But it is necessary to consider precisely what kind of risk is envisaged. When money is borrowed, there is always a certain risk that the debtor will not repay what he owes; the higher the risk, the higher the rate of interest. There have been, from an early stage of modern economics, authors who considered interest largely a payment for risk. Galiani was not all that far removed in time from the late scholastics when he claimed (in an unforgettable phrase) that interest, being the fruit of money, is "the price of the heartbeat" (*il prezzo del batti-*

[13] Scotus, *Sent.*IV,15,2, p.292.
[14] Olivi, f.301va-b; Alexander, p.129.
[15] P.567.

cuore);[16] it is charged by the lender as compensation for the hours of apprehension spent wondering whether he will get his money back.

To insist, then, as Alexander of Hales seems to do, that usury is sinful because a *mutuum*, unlike the lease of a house or some other object, is riskless, may sound rather quaint. However, he is not alluding to the risk of default in repayment, but to the risk of harm or loss occurring to the concrete objects borrowed, viz., in the case of money, to the coins themselves or to the objects bought with the coins. If a house or a horse is lent, ownership remains with the lender, and risk follows ownership. If the house burns down or the horse dies, the loss is the owner's (i.e. the lender's); he cannot demand restitution in the shape of another house or another horse. What he can do, is insure himself in advance by a risk premium in the contract. But if money (or anything else thus loanable) is lent in a *mutuum*, ownership passes and what happens to the money or the goods bought with it is of no concern to the lender. He can ask for his money back anyhow, and to demand a risk premium in addition seems like double payment. A merchant, for instance, who borrows money in order to engage upon some venture, may suffer a loss (physical and/or economic) rather than a gain. Still, he is obliged to repay the loan. In this sense it is riskless on the part of the lender. But suppose the loss ruins the debtor and thus *de facto* nullifies the creditor's legal claim? The reply to this is that even if there is actual default, the contract stands, and equitability refers only to the terms of the contract.

Whether considerations of risk should be said to support the argument from ownership or rather to supplement it, is a matter of taxonomic convenience; they are anyhow related by the assumption that risk normally passes with ownership. Examination of the numerous cases studied by the scholastic doctors where risk plays a major part will undoubtedly reveal that the matter is not always as clear-cut as suggested in the preceding paragraph. Nevertheless, I make bold to leave the risk argument

[16] *Della moneta*, Naples 1750, p.353.

here. It figures prominently in most previous analyses of usury doctrine and is thus already better accounted for elsewhere than is possible within the limited scope of the present monograph. What remains to be said, then, is that considerations of the normal transfer of risk do not fully account for the ownership argument. Even if money is lent in order to be invested in a totally riskless venture (no uncertainty at all attaching to its being repaid fully and in kind at a given future date) the scholastics were committed to arguing that, since ownership passes in a *mutuum*, however the money is spent and whatever profit is made by the borrower are irrelevant to the lender; all he can claim is his money back. The argument from ownership has to be upheld even in this naked form; just as, according to most (if not all) modern economists, interest is a phenomenon (and a numerical rate) to be explained independently of risk.

The retort which presumably springs most readily to the modern mind concerning the scholastic ownership argument against usury, is that it must involve a confusion between ownership of certain pieces of coin and ownership of a certain sum of money in the abstract. It is for the right to use this sum, representing general purchasing power, that the lender pays usury (or interest). Now the medieval mind (as I have argued before and must stress again) was firmly fixed on money in the concrete, and scholastic usury theory was influenced by this fixation, which the discovery of Aristotle's *Politics* did nothing to loosen. Nevertheless, there were some even among the early authors who would conceive of the distinction and admit that the usurer sells not a thing but a *ius*. Henry of Ghent indicated that distinction in a late quodlibetical question,[17] while Gerald Odonis applied it to his refutation of Olivi's positive arguments against usury.[18] In the post-scholastic tradition this would be

[17] *Quodl.*XII,21, f.498r.

[18] F.91v, actually in reply to Olivi's fifth argument. To Olivi's version of the ownership argument (his second) Odonis replies briefly that the creditor does not actually sell a thing belonging to the debtor but that he sells his own indemnity, then adds that the debtor does not necessarily take full ownership.

the end of the whole argument. The right to the use of money is a property right of the lender's, and if it commands a price, it is therefore his to sell. Such is the gist of Molinaeus's reply to the ownership argument.[19] Molinaeus would presumably concede (unlike many subsequent economists) that this *right* would have to be sold at a *just* price, though he does not say so here. To the medieval scholastics this would be the main point, and in the important tradition of usury theory which passed through Bernardino of Siena, this led to what Gerardo of Siena preferred to call, not a *re*jection but a *cor*rection of the ownership argument. One ought not to say, says Gerardo, that a usurious contract is vicious because the usurer acquires a profit which is not his, but because he acquires a profit from something which cannot generate a profit, since it cannot bear fruit.[20] In other words, if money is barren, then the use of money has no just price at all.

Whatever Gerardo of Siena preferred to call it, this is to abandon the ownership argument and to fall back on sterility. That he could do this means (in his case and in the case of those who adopted his line of reasoning) that he believed himself able to show that fungibles are after all barren. This restated proof of sterility is the crux of late usury theory. I must postpone it yet a while, and have anticipated it here merely to indicate the subsequent fate of the ownership argument. Before giving our attention to Gerardo's contribution, it is useful also to follow to their natural conclusions two other analytical developments which took off from the legal foundations described above. Each of them is closely associated with the name of Thomas Aquinas, who entered the usury debate at about the stage to which we had taken it before the last paragraph. Aquinas made several very influential (though perhaps not equally felicitous) suggestions at this point. One of the ensuing analytical developments fol-

19 P.539.

20 Pp.174-5, 179-180; cf. Bernardino of Siena, Sermo 38,1,2, pp.244-6. Bernardino also inserts some remarks of a juridical nature made by Joannes Andreae upon this point in Gerardo's argument; cf. *Quaestiones mercuriales*, f.161ra. Except for such remarks (of less interest to economics), Andreae copied Gerardo's survey of old and new arguments closely and transmitted them to later authors with a canonistic leaning.

lowed in direct prolongation of those sketched above and we can proceed with it here. To the other one we must devote a separate chapter.

If we are to believe Ptolemy of Lucca, Thomas Aquinas may have conceived the idea of his celebrated *Summa theologiae* while in the process of revising his youthful commentary on the *Sentences* of Peter Lombard, a project he then abandoned.[21] Had he persisted, it is at least possible that the old version of that work would have been suppressed by the new. The task of interpreting Aquinas's contributions to the scholastic analysis of usury would then have been at the same time both easier and less satisfying. As it turned out, his early explanation of the *Sentences* kept being copied and subsequently printed in his *Opera* along with the *Summa* as well as a number of other, mostly late works in which he also treats more or less extensively of our subject. If these works are viewed in succession, appearing as they did over a period when the crucial texts of Aristotle were becoming available, one after the other, there is consistency to the development of Aquinas's usury arguments. But if they are taken out of historical context, the whole may seem confusing. There is in particular something that he says in his *Sentences* commentary which may cause an entirely wrong construction to be put on his later works. To avoid doing this, we had better start where the young Thomas himself started.

To understand the economics of Aquinas, one must recall that he was a disciple first of all of Albert the Great, with whom he studied Aristotle's *Ethics* at Cologne before taking up his post as *Sententiarius* at Paris in the 1250's, and that he only became familiar with the *Politics* somewhat later.[22] Following the example of Albert, he disputed a question on usury under Distinction

[21] *Historia Ecclesiastica*,XXIII,15; in *Rerum Italicarum Scriptores*, ed. Muratori, Vol.11, Milan 1727, coll.1172-3.

[22] The datings of some of Aquinas's works are still controversial. Chronology is indicated in note 4 to Chapter 1 above. While Aquinas was among the first to become acquainted with the translations of Aristotle, his own commentaries on the *Ethics* and *Politics* are fairly late works, being more or less contemporaneous with the economic questions of the *Summa theologiae*.

37 of the third book of the *Sentences*. Like his teacher he makes the traditional comparison of money-lending with leasing a house and puts forward three arguments to show the difference, viz. the ownership argument (which both accept), the deterioration argument (which they reject for lack of generality), and a third argument where Thomas also clearly builds on Albert but tries to improve on him.[23] What Albert says is that with the leasing of a house a certain utility passes to the borrower, but not so in a *mutuum*, which ought therefore to be gratis. The latter sounds a little lame, and it is here that Thomas Aquinas makes a notorious remark about money as a measure of value, which has caused some historical interpretations of his contribution to usury doctrine to take off at a tangent.[24]

"All other things have some utility from themselves", says Thomas (clearly echoing Albert the Great) but then adds: "money, however, has not, but is the measure of the utility of other things, which follows from what the Philosopher says in *Ethics*, V." Therefore, usury amounts to "diversifying the measure". Given the inclination of historians to attribute to scholastic economists a conception of money mainly as a legally instituted and fixed value measure, this is an extremely unfortunate way of expressing what Aquinas means here.[25] It should be remembered that when he wrote this, he knew the *Ethics* through Albert the Great but not the *Politics*. The *Ethics* frequently refers to measurement in connection with money, but the point of the analysis where these remarks are made is to define equivalence in economic exchange, and it is clearly this that is foremost in Aquinas's mind. What he seeks to convey (the one way I can understand him) is that in a *mutuum* equivalence consists in paying back exactly what you borrowed, and for that purpose money serves as a correct measure in exchange. If you include a use value, which is fictitious, you diversify the measure. There is nothing here to support the contention that Aquinas considered money value to be immutable in terms of commodities,

[23] Albert, p.708; Thomas, pp.429-430.

[24] Noonan 52; cf. Gordon 163-64, quoting Schumpeter (2) 94.

[25] On the functions of money according to the Aristotelians, see above, pp.63-64.

only that he considered it to be immutable in terms of itself, over the time perspective. In other words, he makes a statement about money in the money market not in the commodity market. Read thus, Aquinas, as well as his teacher Albert the Great, can well be said to anticipate some of the development associated with the names of Olivi and of Gerardo of Siena in particular which will be discussed in Chapter 6. By focusing on the absence of a utility or use value of money they also anticipate the true meaning of the *consumptibility* argument for which Thomas Aquinas is better known.

As soon as he became acquainted with the *Politics*, Aquinas dropped the argument about diversifying the measure, and it was scarcely heard of again in the scholastic tradition. When he wrote about usury again, in *De malo*, in his *Quodlibeta* and in the *Summa theologiae*, he pushed instead another argument, which practically every subsequent usury theorist repeated after him. In order to understand this main Thomist argument it is necessary to put aside all alien ideas about the nature and functions of money. Its whole sense rests on a thoroughly Aristotelian conception of money as set down in the *Politics*: money in the concrete, as coin, made to serve as a medium of exchange. The way the Aristotelians would express this, was to say that the proper use of money was to *commute* or *expend* or *alienate* it, or similar words.[26] To this catalogue the canonist Hostiensis added the verb *consume*: the use of things borrowed in a *locatio* is something different from consumption, but the use of money and other things borrowed in a *mutuum* is to be consumed.[27] If Aquinas had read this, it may have provided the inspiration for his famous consumptibility argument, which in *De malo* runs somewhat as follows.

Usura, says Aquinas, is from *usus*, because a certain price is received for the use of money, as though the use of the money lent is itself sold. But it is to be noted that different things have

[26] Giles of Rome, *De reg. princ.*,II,iii,11, f.222v: *ipsum commutare, vel expendere*, et *alienare*; cf. Astesanus, f.131vb: *distractio pecuniae in commutatione.*

[27] In article *De usuris*, op.cit., col.1280.

different uses. There are some things whose use is the consumption of the substance of those things themselves. Thus the proper use of wine is the drinking of it, and in the process of drinking it the substance of the wine is consumed. Similarly the proper use of wheat or bread is to be eaten, which amounts to the consumption of the wheat or the bread itself. Thus, too, the proper use of money is to be spent in the exchange for other goods: that was the purpose for which money was invented, according to the Philosopher. Then there are certain things whose use is not the consumption of their own substance. Thus a house is used to live in, but one does not live in it in order to demolish it. If it happens that a house in any way improves or deteriorates by being inhabited, this happens by accident, and the same can be said of a horse or a dress and of other things like that. Because such things are not consumed by use as such, it follows that the thing itself or its use may either each be ceded or sold separately or both together; for someone may sell a house, retaining for himself the use of the house for a certain time; and similarly someone may sell the use of the house, retaining ownership of the house for himself. But in the case of those things whose use is consumption, there is no use other than the thing itself; hence to whomever the use of such a thing is conceded, to him is also conceded ownership of the thing, and vice versa. If someone lends money on the agreement that the money be returned and above that will have a certain price for the use of the money, it follows that he sells separately the use of the money and the substance of the money. But the use of money, as was said, is nothing else than its substance; therefore he either sells what does not exist, or sells the same thing twice, which is manifestly contrary to natural justice. The same applies to all those other things whose substance is consumed by use, such as wine, wheat, and the like.[28]

Note first that the function of money as a measure of value is nowhere mentioned in this patient argument (nor in the somewhat briefer restatement of it in the quodlibetical question). The

[28] *De malo*, p.374; cf. *Quodl.*III,19, pp.500-1; *Sum.theol.*, II-II,78,1, p.280.

purpose of money, according to Aquinas, is *ut expendatur pro commutatione*; it is invented *commutationis gratia*. The Philosopher is at first invoked without specific reference. In the version of the *Summa theologiae* both *Ethics*, V and *Politics*, I are cited to the effect that money is for *commutationes faciendas*. This point is not trivial. On the contrary, any reference to the immaterial measurement function of money would have been misleading. To understand what Aquinas's argument here is about, it is necessary to envisage money in material shape; the important thing is what happens to the physical pieces of coin borrowed. Just as wine is drunk and bread is eaten, so coins are spent in exchange. This is what Aquinas means by saying that they are consumed. Nor can there be any doubt that *consumptio* is a synonym for Aristotelian *alienatio*. At least, that is how readers with an Aristotelian leaning would understand Aquinas. Olivi states the consumptibility argument both in reply to the sixth initial objection (this being the horse/house versus money comparison) and as his own third direct argument against usury. Both times copied by Odonis and Bernardino of Siena, Olivi speaks of *consumptio vel alienatio* of money.[29]

It does not look, however, as though the argument from consumptibility is at first inspired by Aristotle. I would see it rather as an attempt to improve on the dominant canonistic argument from ownership. Even if money is taken in a concrete sense, this argument is not wholly satisfactory, since it rests on nothing but a legal definition. What Aquinas tries to do is to show that usury is wrong because of what *must* normally happen to money borrowed in a *mutuum*. Ownership of the actual coins borrowed must necessarily pass because some other pieces of coin are to be paid back. In the version of the consumptibility argument quoted above, this is not stated expli-

[29] Olivi, f.301vb, 303va; cf. Odonis, f.90v, 93r; Bernardino, Sermo 36,3,6, p.215, Sermo 38,1,3, p.246. Olivi's juxtaposition of these terms may be due to Henry of Ghent; cf. *Quodl.*I,39, f.25v. Others who repeated the consumptibility argument include Astesanus, f.130vb; Pisanus, f.185rb-va; Richard of Middleton, *Sent.*IV,15,5,5, pp.223b-224a; Durandus of Saint-Pourçain, *Sent.* III,37,2, f.281ra; Antonino of Florence, *Summa*,II,i,6,1, coll.75-6; Angelus, f.363va; Trovamala, f.247rb-va.

citly, but it comes through more clearly in later versions. Both in the quodlibetical question and in the *Summa*, Aquinas explains that in the case of things loanable in a *mutuum*, their use consumes their substance, and *therefore*, he concludes, ownership passes. Usury is not sinful because ownership passes; that would sit too loosely as the premise of a moral theory. Ownership must pass because of the way money is intended to be used. What makes usury wrong is the counting of substance and use separately, considering that money is spent immediately in use.

Another canonistic principle also comes up for revision, namely the distinction between things which do and do not deteriorate in use. As will be recalled, Aquinas had rejected the argument that objects legitimately leased for profit are such as do not deteriorate, on the ground that it is not generally valid. In *De malo* he repeats the objection (fourth argument in favour of usury) that a horse or a house can be profitably lent; why not money? He again cites the non-deterioration argument only to reject it. It would mean, says Aquinas, that the charge would be limited to the actual deterioration.[30] In the body of his own analysis, as quoted, it is admitted that improvement or deterioration can happen accidentally, but when a parallel is then drawn with money, the old distinction is as it were reversed. Far from remaining intact compared with houses or horses, money not only deteriorates in use, it is consumed and completely gone. In his quodlibetical question Aquinas invites the same comparison between money which is normally *consumed* and other objects which are *destroyed* in use at most accidentally, as though these words were synonyms.[31]

In modern economics the antonym to consumption is of course investment, and there is possibly also something in Aquinas's treatment which invites the condemnation of consumption as against investment loans, although this is clearly not his intention. Since the particular utility derived from the object of a contract by one party to it can be no legitimate source

[30] P.375.
[31] P.500.

of profit to the other party[32] (and since in a *mutuum* ownership passes anyhow), the scholastic principles of justice provide no basis for a distinction between different uses of borrowed money. Nevertheless, there must have been a strong emotional inclination to judge loans for consumption more severely than loans for investment perhaps promising a large profit to the debtor. When Aquinas speaks of consumption and takes comestibles for his examples, he seems to appeal to this inclination. If you borrow food and wine and besides returning equal quantities of food and wine are required to pay for their use (which is to eat and drink them), you certainly seem to pay for something which does not exist or to pay for the same thing twice. Now introducing Aristotle into this picture, the striking feature is that he tends to speak of the purpose of money as that of being a medium in the exchange of *necessaries*, with which one would of course normally associate consumption goods.

If, instead of borrowing food and wine, you borrow money in order to buy food and wine, it seems almost equally unreasonable to make you pay for its use. Whether consumption is immediate in terms of necessaries or one or two links away from them in the chain of exchanges, does not seem to make much difference in principle. It would probably be hard for the medieval reader of Aquinas's consumptibility argument to liberate himself from this association. It is all the more important, therefore, to arrest it as irrelevant. What defines money as a consumptible in his employment of the word is not the fact that it initiates a chain of exchanges which eventually results in something to be consumed; rather it is the fact that it is exchanged at all rather than kept. Alienation makes it a consumptible immediately, in its first exchange, for whatever object. If a merchant borrows money in order to invest it in some business venture calculated to return a profit above the principal, it is clearly consumed in a very different sense from the sense in which food and wine (or money for food and wine) are consumed, but it is nonetheless consumed in the Thomist sense. The merchant still has his money (and more, if he is lucky) and can

[32] See above, p.47, 50.

pay it back, if only in kind. But the physical pieces of coin borrowed are gone and thus consumed.

To recapitulate, then, what the Thomist argument says is that if you use money (the way it is intended to be used) you immediately consume its substance, hence if you pay for its use having already paid for its substance, you pay twice for the same thing or you pay for something (the use) which does not exist separately from the substance. The objection to this kind of reasoning from a modern point of view would again be that it is led astray by a focus on money in the concrete, money as a substance. Even though this substance slips out of your hands immediately you put money to use (today you often don't even touch this substance in the first place), you have initiated an economic process by means of money in the abstract; this process is the use of money in the relevant sense, and its profits ought to be shared by the lender. This objection was anticipated by Molinaeus. The use and fruition of money, says this sixteenth-century author in objection to St Thomas's consumptibility argument, does not consist only in its first momentary spending but also in the succeeding use of the goods or things purchased with the money.[33] I quote Molinaeus in order to bring into the open what really underlies the modern objection. It seems to say that if you had consumed money the way you consume food, the argument might be valid, but because you actually "consume" it into a process where it yields a fruit, therefore it does not hold.

When Gerardo of Siena "corrected" the argument from consumptibility, what he brought to its support (just as in the case of the ownership argument) was the sterility of money. You may well transfer money (or any fungible) as a substance separately from the use to which it is to be put until the date of its repayment in kind (i.e. in a different substance), but because this use can yield no fruit however you spend money and whatever process you initiate with it, therefore this substance and this use, though logically separate, are *one value*, and if you pay for both you still pay twice or pay for something (a use

[33] P.539.

value) which does not exist.[34] The precise argument must wait until we have seen how Gerardo demonstrates sterility.[35] To conclude for the time being, the gist of these objections to Aquinas is that use cannot be said to be the same as substance; the real question is whether there exists a use *value* of money besides its substantive *value*.

Now Aquinas's original formulations may well be read in terms of value. What he condemns, is taking "a certain price for the use of money". To object that use is not substance then becomes mere verbal quibble. As far as I can see, Aquinas only once stated in conventional terms that money is sterile, namely in his Gloss on Luke, where he quotes a crude "barren metal" statement of Gregory of Nyssa.[36] That was just before he composed *De malo*. The consumptibility argument then became his particular way of stating the sterility argument.[37] Some subsequent users saw the connection. Thus Astesanus deduced the condemnation of Aristotelian *tokos* directly from Aquinas.[38] That it was present in Aquinas's own mind is evident where he makes more casual references to consumptibility. Thus, not long before he stopped writing, Aquinas commented on the fourteenth Psalm, one of the central Old Testament loci on usury doctrine. Citing the injunction against lending at usury, he quotes his own conclusion in his own characteristic phrase (viz. that the usurer "sells what does not exist") with an addition: ... *vendit quod non est, cum non habeat usumfructum.*[39] This is Aquinas's last word on usury, and it is a simple assertion of the dogma that money does not bear fruit.

[34] Gerardo, pp.175-6, p.180; cf. Andreae, f.161ra-va, 162rb; Bernardino, Sermo 38,1,3, p.247. Odonis also criticizes the Thomist argument. In reply to Olivi's third argument against usury (which is the consumptibility argument), Odonis states (f.91v) that the use and the substance of money can indeed be separated. The difference between a *mutuum* and a *locatio* is then mainly a question of who carries the risk.

[35] See below, p.119 ff.

[36] P. 74.

[37] While I must sometimes differ from Noonan's interpretations, on this point we are at one. About Aquinas's argument, Noonan remarks (56): "sterility is really the same as consumptibility".

[38] F.130vb; cf. also Hassia, f.196ra.

[39] *Postilla super Psalmos*, p.187; cf. *Sum.theol.*,II-II,78,3, p.282.

5. Money and industry

If a poor man borrows money in order to buy food or other necessaries which he then proceeds to consume, it is easy to argue that money is fruitless, since there is no fruit to be accounted for. But if an artisan or a merchant borrows money in order to invest in his trade and thereby makes a profit, how is this profit to be accounted for if money is barren? It can and must be accounted for, said the scholastics, fully and completely, by *human industry.* Whenever the question arose, this served as the standard answer. It may not have been wholly satisfactory even in the early centuries while objections to orthodox doctrine were largely rhetorical. When usury doctrine came under serious attack, those defenders of it who relied on human industry to explain all profit found themselves driven to some rather questionable reasoning. We shall have to show in our concluding chapters that the sterility argument in its mature form does not really depend on such reasoning. To this end it is necessary to devote the present chapter to recording the original arguments about the fruitfulness of industry and to demonstrating what they led to.

The positive doctrine is stated by Thomas Aquinas in his youthful commentary on the *Sentences*. Expressing the sentiments of the creditor, he argues in opposition to accepted teaching as follows: Since I may hope for something even from those whom I have done no service, should I not all the more be allowed to hope for something from those who have benefited from me, *in casu* by borrowing my money? The argument is invalid, says Aquinas, for any utility experienced by the receiver of money comes from "the industry of him who wisely uses the money", and this industry cannot be sold to him by the money-lender.[1] In the *Summa theologiae*, the reference to *industria* is appended to the description of goods whose use is their consumption, and which have no usufruct, in that that which is acquired via such goods is not properly the fruit of those goods but rather of human industry.[2]

The context in which this explanation is given in the *Summa*, is one in which many subsequent scholastics used it or discussed it. It concerns the restitution of ill-gotten gains, and Aquinas addresses a delicate problem raised by the further employment of money earned by usury. Within this context the reference to *industria* had in fact been made before Aquinas.

Suppose a lender has received back a sum B in excess of the principal A and is to make restitution. It is clear that he can normally keep A (which was his in the first place) but must return B, deduction having been made for legitimate claims under extrinsic titles. Thus the lender may have suffered a loss by lending (*damnum emergens*), or instead of lending he might have employed the money in question otherwise and thus not forgone a profit (*lucrum cessans*). Originating in Roman law, such extrinsic titles came gradually to be acknowledged in the course of the historical period under observation here.[3] Suppose, however, that the erstwhile lender, before being brought to book, has had the chance to invest B in some legitimate economic venture and thereby makes a profit C in excess of B. The question then, which posed a real dilemma for the usury theorists, is this: Is it now sufficient to return B to the former borrower, or should the profit C be returned as well?[4]

William of Auxerre in his *Summa aurea* examined the question of restitution of profit derived from money extracted by

[1] *Sent.*III,37,1,6, p.429, 430.

[2] II-II,78,3, p.282.

[3] For the relation of this principle to the first half of St Thomas's "double rule" of just pricing in commodity exchange, see above, p.50.

[4] In order to visualize the dilemma in a contemporary context, consider the story of the executive who, entrusted with a large consignment of his company's funds, makes some fast foreign exchange speculations which earn him a profit before converting the funds and delivering them to their proper recipient. Question: Is this profit truly his or should it be returned to his employer?

usury and concluded that all (C as well as B) is to be returned, for B is the root of C, and if the root is dead so is the branch. Excepted, however, is that which may be retained by the usurer *pro labore et industria sua.*[5] The root simile seems singularly inappropriate within a theory invoking the sterility of money. Even if deductions are being granted for what is earned by industry there must presumably in the normal case be something left over, otherwise there would be no problem, and this something must have its origin in money. Dead or not, the root evidently sprouts a branch. Nevertheless, William's teaching was confirmed by Raymond of Peñafort several decades later in his very influential summary for confessors. According to this author, restitution must be made for C, after deducting for the usurer's expenses *et forte operas suas moderatas.*[6]

It follows from what was said above, that unless the latter title is to be extended materially so as in principle to wipe out C, this is dangerous teaching since it seems to overturn the basic tenet of usury doctrine that no money can legitimately be made by money as such. It is not impossible on William's and Raymond's principles for the original borrower to earn money in that way. Having scraped together enough to pay the usurer (the sum B together with the principal A) and entertaining no alternative plans for the money thus lost, he suddenly finds, through the repentance and restitution of the lender, that he has made a profit without lifting a finger. This criticism was made by John Duns Scotus discussing restitution in his commentary on the *Sentences.* Profit on objects which truly fructify is to be given the one who is unjustly deprived of such objects, says Scotus, but profit acquired by money is not to be returned to the borrower from whom that money was originally extracted by means of usury, lest the borrower become *iuste usurarius,* which cannot be permitted.[7]

To justify this conclusion, Scotus (like numerous subsequent writers subscribing to it) fell back on Thomist *industria.* In fact,

[5] *Summa,*III,21, f.226rb.
[6] Pp.242-3.
[7] *Sent.*IV,15,2, p.333.

although he does not refer specifically to either William of Auxerre or to Raymond of Peñafort, considerations similar to those voiced by Scotus may well have motivated Thomas Aquinas in subtly changing the tenor of the original solution. While William is prepared to deduct something under the title of industry, Aquinas will have industry account for everything. How much difference his absolute rejection of any claim to profit on money, compared to the conditional affirmation implied by earlier teaching, will make in practical application, depends on how inclusive the compensation for expenses (including labour) can be made from case to case. It may come to the same thing. But in principle the difference is significant. Aquinas plugs a loophole left open by William of Auxerre in the "root" argument. That simile does not fit, says Aquinas. A root possesses not only the nature of a material cause, such as money may be said to be in the case of profit made by usurious gains, it also possesses the nature of an active cause, in that it administers nutriment, and money does not do this. In other words, money is barren, the root is truly dead. There can be no question of deducting something for expenses and perhaps something under other titles and imputing the balance to money. On the contrary, money, admittedly necessary to gain as an instrumental cause, can lay claim to none of this gain; only human industry, as the principal cause, can do this.[8]

Aquinas's solution is perhaps open to the objection that it might tempt a lender to demand usury, make a quick profit on the proceeds, repent and restitute B and then sit back and enjoy C cleared of all sin. Ridolfi, considering some such possibility, recommended that the lender, while perhaps not obliged to return this gain to the borrower (in view of Scotus's counter-objection), ought rather to give it to the poor, since it would be usurious on his own part as well.[9] In the context of early usury theory the latter objection may be valid. However, as the doc-

[8] *Sum.theol.*, loc.cit. A similar argument is to be found already in Aquinas's quodlibetical question on usury (p.501), but the specific reference to industry does not occur there.

[9] F.24vb.

trine developed and the titles of *lucrum cessans* were extended and came to be more generally acknowledged, the objection may have tended to lose some of its force. Aquinas in fact adds the stipulation that if the original borrower was hurt by being deprived of the money he had to repay above the principal, then an estimate of this loss can be deducted from what the lender can claim as the fruit of his industry (in subsequently making the profit C).[10] If this principle is extended to include potential forgone gain by deprivation of the means of evincing industry on the borrower's part, there will be a surplus on the usurer's part only in so far as his industry is truly more profitable than the borrower's industry. A position is then reached which seems to conform more or less with what was eventually established in direct analysis of usury rather than restitution.

An impressive list can be made of authors who attributed profit to human industry in connection with restitution of illegitimate economic gains.[11] Meanwhile, the principle was used in positive argumentation against usury. Most popular was a verbal tradition originating in Scotus's *Sentences* commentary, where it represents his third argument against usury (following Aquinas's consumptibility argument and the legal argument about the transfer of ownership). Clearly inspired again by Aquinas, the Franciscan teacher asserts that "money does not of its nature have any fruit, as have other things that germinate of themselves, but any fruit (in connection with money) grows of someone's industry, viz. the user's".[12] Versions of this statement are to be found in numerous later authors.[13] It

[10] *Sum.theol.*, loc.cit.

[11] It would include names like Richard of Middleton, *Sent.*IV, 15,5,6, p.224b; Astesanus, f.139rb; Pisanus, f.190ra; Antonino of Florence, *Summa*,II,ii,2,5, col.374; Francis of Platea, f.118v; Gabriel Biel, *Sent.*IV,15,11, f.QQ_3 vb.

[12] P.293.

[13] Cf., for instance, Astesanus, f.130vb; Biel, f.PP_6va. One of those who followed Scotus closely on this subject was Nider, whose treatise "On the Contracts of Merchants" is not only the first one of its kind ever to be printed (see note 12 to Chapter 1) but also the only one so far to be translated into English. I quote the relevant section from Nider *in extenso*: "Nevertheless, money does not have of its own nature any capacity, as some other things have, of inherent fertility. Any return originates in the industry of someone else, who is

will not surprise the reader to learn that slight variation in this type of statement might fatefully alter its purport. It is money that has to be explained away. It is there, in collaboration with industry, and since it obviously has some kind of causal character, it can easily slip through and assume a more active role. We shall return to this presently.[14]

Among the various traditions concerning the fruitfulness of human industry employing barren money, there is one which is of particular interest to the present study, namely the tradition which passed through the important work of Bernardino of Siena. No doubt it also originated in the works of Aquinas and Scotus, but it received its verbal form in the treatise by Peter Olivi. Before stating his own natural law case against usury consisting of seven positive arguments in favour of the prohibition, Olivi records nine traditional objections to the prohibition, all in a sense arguments in favour of permitting usury. Some of them pretend to build on natural law as well. Olivi counters them in conclusion of his main question (before turning to cases in his *dubia*). Both in one of his own arguments against usury and in reply to two of the traditional arguments in favour of usury, Olivi invokes *industria*.

The very first objection to the prohibition of usury which he cites is evidently built on Aquinas in his commentary on the *Sentences*: Money borrowed confers a certain advantage upon him who receives it; therefore according to natural equity, it may be compensated. This argument is not valid, according to Olivi, for the advantage which money seems to confer has in reality its fount solely in the *operatio* and *industria* of the borrower.[15] A closely related objection and answer are to be found in the treatise by Odonis, who agrees fully with Olivi

employing the money – not the loaner. Since the industry of the debtor is not that of him who grants the loan, by wishing to receive interest on the money, the latter wants to have a return from industry which is not his and which is not properly due to him from the debtor". (C.H.Reeves's translation, Norman, Oklahoma 1966, p.51).

14 See below, p.105 and note 43.

15 Olivi, f.300rb, 302va.

here.[16] Bernardino of Siena quotes Olivi practically verbatim in his thirty-sixth economic sermon.[17] This is Bernardino's "first defence" of usury and its rejection. Similarly, in connection with his "sixth defence" of usury, Bernardino copies Olivi's statement and rejection of the sixth reason cited by him in favour of permitting usury. It is also in Odonis. The objection here reaches all the way back to *Eiciens*: why is the lending of a house or a horse for gain permitted and not of money? Because, says Olivi, in those goods, use and fruit differ from consumption; moreover, this use does not arise solely from the *actus* and *industria* of the user.[18] In both these replies by Olivi much of the interest lies in the words he couples with industry, thereby indicating what industry means. We shall pick up this thread again very shortly.

Olivi also invokes the sterility of money in one of his own direct natural law arguments against usury, namely his fourth, where he says that to sell somebody his own industry is unjust, and that is precisely what the usurer does, since money confers no profit except *per industriam*.[19] This was copied by Bernardino, constituting his seventh argument (of a total of twelve) to show that usury is against natural law; and by Antonino of Florence through Bernardino.[20] As mentioned in the survey of sources, Odonis also copies Olivi's natural law arguments against usury, but only in order to take them apart.[21] In the case of the fourth argument cited above, his criticism does not demolish but rather strengthens the industry principle, in that it points to an extension of the principle which was to prove

[16] Odonis, f.90r, 92r. This is the second argument in favour of usury cited and answered by Odonis.

[17] Bernardino, Sermo 36,3,1, pp.209-210.

[18] Olivi, f.300va, 303rb-va; Odonis (eighth argument and answer), f.90v, 93r; Bernardino, Sermo 36,3,6, pp.215-6.

[19] Olivi, f.301vb.

[20] Bernardino, Sermo 38,1,7, pp.250-1; cf. Antonino, *Summa*, II,i,6,1, col.76. It is probably the same general tradition which speaks in Martin Luther's somewhat confused reference in his Table Talks to the sterility of money and the non-vendibility of *industria*. (Luther, *Werke, Tischreden*, Vol.IV (1916), No.4805 at p.524; Vol.V (1919), No.5429 at p.146).

[21] See above, pp.29-30.

crucial at a much later stage. It is not correct to say that the lender sells the borrower the latter's industry, says Odonis. Rather, he sells the "cessation of his own industry". While beneficial to the borrower, this cessation is harmful to the lender, for "both cannot use the money at once".[22]

If this had been written as much as two centuries later, it might still be registered as an interesting, brief statement of a slightly avant-garde position; written in the early fourteenth century it is truly remarkable. Odonis here foreshadows the justification of *lucrum cessans* by a quite general reference to being deprived of the opportunity to use scarce money. Bernardino (who wrote more than a century afterwards) has been praised for doing exactly that, but there can be no doubt that the fifteenth-century preacher in adopting this line relied on his earlier highly respected confrère. Discussing *lucrum cessans* in his forty-first sermon, Bernardino states that "money has value not from itself, but from its owner's industry, and therefore the receiver of the money not only deprives the owner of his money, but of all the use and fruit of exercising his industry in it and through it".[23] The English wording is that of Noonan, who describes this answer as "exceedingly astute", being the only logically possible way of preserving the sterility of money in the face of this kind of objection.[24] I would personally prefer to emphasize the doctrinal consistency of the answer and point out that it goes way back in time before Bernardino of Siena, to an early scholastic writer who maintained the creditor's justifiable claim to compensation for enforced idleness throughout his treatise on usury. When this bit of textual criticism is corrected, it may perhaps be added that to make an issue of how far individual authors at different points in time acknowledged extrinsic titles is a little beside the real point of usury doctrine. What counts in connection with the development and survival of the scholastic doctrine is not *whose* industry is at stake: the lender's, or the borrower's. What counts is rather the *nature* of

[22] Odonis, ff.90v-91r, f.91v.
[23] Bernardino, Sermo 41,1,3, p.315.
[24] Noonan 126-7.

human industry as a productive factor and, more specifically, the nature of its admittedly fruitful relationship to money.

It was mentioned in the opening chapters of this study that the early modern students of scholastic economics believed themselves able to establish a unity between the doctrine of just commodity pricing and the doctrine of interest and usury on money, in that a peculiar labour theory of value was seen as representing the foundation of both doctrines.[25] In the case of commodity exchange, the labour interpretation was based on the acknowledged principle that the seller must be permitted to keep himself indemnified for actual costs incurred, as well as on the frequent reference to "labour and expenses" as an estimate of just equivalence between exchangers. This phrase was popularized in the Aristotelian commentary tradition by Albert the Great and continued, throughout that tradition, to play an important role as a handy criterion of fairness. Similarly, in the case of money-lending, the principle of indemnity which underlay acknowledgement of the extrinsic titles could be read as expressing a labour theory. Finally, to return to the topic presently at issue, the references to industry rather than money as the source of profit seemed to round off this harmonious picture very nicely. When the interpretation underlying it came to be abandoned in the case of commodity pricing, remnants of it might tend to nourish the misconception of a conflict between a market theory of the just price and an archaic labour theory still prevailing in the case of usury, thus preventing this area of economics from developing as fruitfully as the other main area was about to do. This picture is inaccurate. In order to clear the path to where the doctrines really differ, it is necessary to show here why the industry theory of usury (at least as it appears in the Olivian tradition) is not in any relevant sense a labour theory. Two considerations effectively rule out the possibility of using that description with any accuracy in the present instance.

First, the scholastic theory of usury is not the kind of labour

[25] See above, pp.15-16, and p.51.

theory (of value and/or of distribution) to which the term was to be applied in later centuries, i.e. a theory which contrasts labour and real capital. In the critical tradition from Summenhart through Molinaeus, one of the objections regularly raised against attributing the fruits of money to industry was that the same would apply to a field or a house or indeed to any of the objects which the scholastics did consider fruit-bearing; for they don't normally bear fruit either, without the interference of human industry.[26] The scholastics were adamant in claiming that there was a difference. If a thing which fructifies is removed from the owner by unlawful means, the fruit (perhaps, it is true, after deduction for industry) is to be returned with the object itself; if money is removed, all that is to be returned is sterile money. Aquinas states this in the case of restitution of profit on usurious money in the *Summa theologiae*, in fact taking a field and a house as his examples.[27] In the Olivi-Bernardino axis, it is a house or a horse as opposed to money.[28] It is not only that these objects fall under different classes of contracts, but that they must do so because one class of objects is fruitful (or at least useful) while the other is sterile, *industria* accounting for all increment. What is contrasted is not industry versus real capital but industry and real capital of all kinds versus money. This is maintained so uncompromisingly that the scholastics ran head-on into a rather obvious objection levelled against them by the first post-scholastic critics and still voiced with exasperation by historians: How could this doctrine possibly be valid in view of the fact that money in the borrower's hand is often immediately converted into fruit-bearing capital – and in fact borrowed for that express purpose?

Second, the industry theory is a labour theory only to the extent that *industria* actually meant labour, and labour hardly covers the full meaning of the word as used by the scholastics in this connection. In the discussion about the origins of capitalism centred on the Weber thesis, the history of the concept of

[26] Summenhart, Q.23, ad 2, p.88; Molinaeus, p.540.
[27] Loc.cit.
[28] See above, p.97 and sources cited in note 18.

industria naturally played a part. I am not about to reopen that issue here. Suffice it to say that Weber himself would take the origin of the concept back to "monastic asceticism", where the emphasis on industry in the sense of *assiduity* would of course be predominant.[29] Assiduity is not primarily a business skill or virtue. Be that as it may; it is clear that the concept throughout the centuries which followed and during which it was applied to usury doctrine, did not always mean the same thing to all authors. When William of Auxerre, discussing restitution, speaks of *labor* and *industria* in one breath, he may not have intended any significant distinction between them.[30] Olivi, copied by Bernardino, also used that combination but sometimes used different combinations as well.

I have just recorded some instances of this. There are some other instances in one of the questions about value and price preceding his analysis of usury in the triple treatise. Olivi is much concerned there with the factors which give rise to value in a commodity (or a service – he is also interested in the question of the just wage) to justify sellers' price claims. In this connection the human cost element to Olivi is not only labour, but labour with a difference: a skill acquired by nature or by education, even an initiative. In two successive examples, Olivi refers to human industry. In one of them he explains how one product is worth more than another owing to more *labor et industria*, making no point of a possible difference of meaning. Before that, however, while discussing a building project, he remarks that he who quarries and cuts the stones, although he puts in more bodily effort, is paid less than the architect who guides and instructs the labourers with higher *peritia* (practical knowledge and skill) *et industria*. On the same page Olivi also relates *peritia* and *industria* to *sollicitudo mentalis*. Bernardino of Siena copied all these phrases.[31]

It is unquestionable that Olivi had a particularly keen eye for

29 Weber 202.

30 See above, p.93.

31 Olivi, Siena BC U.V.6, f.296vb; ed. Spicciani, p.259; cf. Bernardino, Sermo 35,2,2-3, p.198. See also Langholm (1) 155-6.

such nuances, and it is largely owing to him that they were so clearly accentuated in the subsequent tradition attributing the fruits of commercial activities to a human agent. On the other hand, the particular aspect of human industry which Olivi brought to the fore and which authors in the Bernardino line communicated to modern critics was latent in the tradition from the very start. Note, for instance, that Thomas Aquinas in his commentary on the *Sentences* attributes profit not to labour but to him who uses money wisely (*sagaciter*).[32] As any medieval Latin word list will confirm, *industria* can carry the various meanings indicated above. It embraces *diligence* and *assiduity*, but also *sagacity, cleverness, shrewdness.* These are business skills. Gordon goes the whole distance; explaining the position of Bernardino he renders *industria* as "entrepreneurship".[33] In doing so, Gordon is in the tradition of Werner Sombart, the German historian and critic of Max Weber who popularized the notion of the capitalistic sympathies of the fifteenth-century Tuscan saints. For *industria*, Sombart used the word "Unternehmungsgeist", literally "the spirit of entrepreneurship".[34] Is not this in fact "the spirit of capitalism" itself? Anyhow, to conclude this philological excursion: If its findings are correct, the scholastic "labour" theory of usury is a theory which lumps together the entrepreneur with the labourer, and to which that particular label is perhaps therefore – in view of certain subsequent ideological developments – best not applied.

Terminology apart, it is clear that if *industria* can be taken as close to *entrepreneurship* as some scholars suggest, it may invite a conception of the relation between money and human industry which can quite easily cause the scholastic edifice to topple in an unintended direction. It means that what can legitimately account for profit in business enterprise is not toil and trouble but the application of a particular acumen and know-how to money. If this point of view is adopted, it is simple for the idea to assert itself that it is not in fact the human factor

[32] See above, p.91.
[33] Gordon 198, n.22.
[34] Sombart 321.

alone which bears fruit directly. If it can be said to do so at all, it is at least partly by indirect means that it bears fruit, namely by means of money. Or more correctly, it is partly money which bears fruit, but the entrepreneur is required (so to speak) to inseminate money. It is not that money is needed in order for human diligence to become fruitful (as scholastics in the Thomist tradition undoubtedly mostly thought of it), but rather that human sagacity is needed in order for money to become fruitful. *Industry fructifies money*. This is what Summenhart and Molinaeus said after having pointed out that man is necessary for a field to bear fruit as well:[35] "Thus also money bears fruit, i.e. becomes profitable, if man uses it in exchange" (Summenhart); "money likewise yields a product through the industry of man" (Molinaeus). Long after the scholastic era was over, statements of this kind can be found in economic texts like echoes of an old battle. Consider, for instance, the following explanation of profit given by Francis Hutcheson, Adam Smith's first teacher of economics (my emphases): "Houses yield no fruits or increase, nor will some arable grounds yield any without great labour. Labour employed *in managing money* in trade, or manufactures, *will make it as fruitful* as any thing".[36]

Now it so happens that some of the late scholastics can be made out to say almost precisely the same thing, and this apparent twist to inherited doctrine naturally came to play a pivotal part in the very opinionated discussion of the possible Catholic roots of Weberian capitalism. There is particularly one statement of this nature which has come to figure prominently in that discussion. For some reason all critics who quote it (each typically copying a previous one without return to sources) attribute it to Antonino of Florence,[37] while in fact Antonino, here as so often elsewhere, simply quotes Bernardino who quotes Olivi – here as so often elsewhere – but this time in his *Quodlibeta* and not in his economic treatise. In discussing a

[35] See above, p.100 and references in note 26.

[36] *A System of Moral Philosophy*,II,13, London 1755, Vol.II, p.72.

[37] It seems that the statement was originally located in Antonino's *Summa* in Funk (2) 151; I have found it repeated after him in Brants 134, Rambaud 41, Sombart 511, Hauser 60, and O'Brien 181.

case pertaining to usury Olivi lets fall this remark that money is not of itself alone (*ex se sola*) profitable, *sed ex industria mercantium fit per eorum negotitiones lucrosa.*[38]

Industry fructifies ("befruchtet") money, says Sombart explaining this phrase,[39] for once agreeing with Weber, according to whom Antonino of Florence had already refuted the doctrine of the sterility of money.[40] Had anybody before Calvin discovered that money begets money, asks Hauser, referring to Antonino of Florence but comforting himself in the assurance that this "isolated affirmation" had no apparent effect on the subsequent development of ideas.[41] Even Schumpeter was impressed by Antonino's performance. He finally enabled the scholastics to "block out a theory of the role in production and commerce of monetary capital", says Schumpeter. Antonino "explained that though the circulating coin might be sterile, money capital is not so because command of it is a condition for embarking upon business". In a footnote to the latter statement he remarks: "This, of course, was a frontal attack on Aristotle's 'sterility of money'".[42]

A main motive for my heavy documentation of the arguments about industry in the present chapter was to place the reader in a position to judge for himself about the late scholastics' so-called attack on Aristotle. Whatever is to be read into the quotation which provoked these comments, the historical circumstances are clear. It is not the Dominican archbishop of Renaissance Florence who says this but a Franciscan heretic much farther removed in time from Antonino than from the *poverello* himself. Antonino cannot have felt that he was saying anything extraordinary. He was simply copying a statement that had survived for centuries in the tradition side by side with other ways of expressing accepted dogma. The remarkable thing is that it could so survive. There is nothing to indicate that Olivi

38 Olivi, *Quodl.*I,17, ed. Venice c.1505, f.7va; cf. Bernardino, Sermo 42,2,1, p.357; Antonino, *Summa*,II,i,7,16, col.99.

39 Sombart 321.

40 Weber 83.

41 Hauser, loc.cit.

42 Schumpeter (2) 101, 105.

wants to repudiate Aristotelian principles. But the kind of statement which he makes (and others repeat after him) is clearly invited in virtue of the position which the scholastics had chosen to occupy. If fruits are due to industry but money is somehow needed for industry to assert itself, it is almost unavoidable for someone sooner or later to cross the line and say that industry fructifies money. How significant is this slip of the tongue? A later historical perspective would see it as significant. Perhaps it was, even to the scholastics, a more natural way of expressing the true relationship, suppressed by orthodoxy but subconsciously breaking out? However, little is gained by letting this kind of historico-psychological speculation run wild. If the scholastics said that money is sterile, perhaps it would be best to take their arguments for this at face value until deliberately countered, rather than permitting hindsight to squeeze new meaning out of them.[43]

[43] Before leaving this particular subject, and in order to underscore my point further, I would like to give another example of a statement apparently refuting the sterility dogma quite as directly as does the one attributed to Antonino of Florence, and likewise going back almost to the time of Peter Olivi. For some reason it has escaped the attention of historians, though it appears in a much published book. As mentioned above (see p.95), one of the most frequently repeated versions of the proposition that profit is due to industry and not money is that of John Duns Scotus. It was copied by Astesanus in his *Summa* for confessors, one of the most popular books of its kind, which saw at least ten editions before 1500. If the ordinary working moralist, so to speak, came across Scotus's formulation, it is much more likely to have been via Astesanus's handbook than in the tomes of the *doctor subtilis.* Most other disciples of Scotus quoted him more or less verbatim. In the original the lines quoted from Scotus above read as follows. *Pecunia non habet ex natura sua aliquem fructum . . ., sed tantum provenit aliquis fructus ex industria alterius, scilicet utentis.* The meaning is quite clear: money is barren, industry accounts for all fruit. But Astesanus abbreviates, thereby changing the meaning radically: *Nullum fructum habet pecunia ex sua natura sed tantum ex utentis industria.* (Money does not have any fruit from its nature but only from the user's industry.) This is to say that industry fructifies money just as openly as does Olivi's statement. I cannot imagine that Astesanus would deliberately go against Scotus, one of the greatest acknowledged teachers of his order, even by thus trying to surpass him in verbal subtlety. There may be other similar examples in the early sources. Why have they not been found before? Availability is not the whole answer; Astesanus is certainly available. Another part of the truth may well be that no one has been looking for this kind of statement in an early author. In Astesanus it would be a little embarrassing. In Antonino it is a small sensation.

Unfortunately for the scholastics, one of the arguments which some of them used in connection with industry to prove that money is indeed barren, could easily be turned against them and used to prove that the statement quoted from Olivi above must in fact have the meaning which posterity has read into it. In order to explain this line of the tradition, we must once more go back to *Eiciens* and even beyond it.[44] As will be recalled, the second reason put forward there to show why lending a field or a house for profit can be permitted while lending money cannot is that the former kinds of property may yield a profit to the owner, whereas "from money laid up you get no benefit". This was understood by the early scholastics to refer to the sterility of money. Innocent IV, one of the last to discuss economics without the aid of Aristotle, invoked *Eiciens* as his authority for that principle,[45] and this became common usage. The reasoning seems to be that while a field will be worked on and a house inhabited if it remains in the possession of the potential lender, money will on the contrary lie idle. In fact, the anonymous Latin version of this text which the *palea* paraphrases is even more explicit. It states that you get no benefit from money laid up with you *in sacculo*. If the usurer, instead of lending money to someone who needs it, had kept it shut up *in a bag*, he would have earned nothing from it anyhow, and so should ask nothing from the borrower. This meaning seems to be to some extent preserved in the abbreviated version more familiar to the scholastics, and conformed well with their own intention. It was by proving that money would in fact not have lain idle in the hand of the potential lender, but that he would rather have used it as a necessary condition for exercising his own industry, that *lucrum cessans* could be claimed.

However, in the context of Aristotelian economics it is clear that what happens to money *in the bag* is not very relevant. Money was invented in order to serve as a medium of exchange, and the scholastics following Aristotle had to argue that money

[44] As background for the discussion in this paragraph, see the quotation on p.72 above, with references in note 4, as well as some remarks on pp.73-74.

[45] Innocent, *Decr.*V,39,48, f.556vb.

was *sterile even out of the bag*. By a strange irony, it is when remaining in the bag that it may sometimes be permitted to yield a fruit. It will be remembered that the scholastics conceded that money may be a legitimate object of a profitable *locatio* rather than a *mutuum*.[46] In other words, coins may be borrowed and the identical coins returned, ownership remaining with the lender. Who would borrow money on this condition? The examples provided by the scholastics were of those who borrowed money (or other valuables) as security or for ostentation. Profit on money thus handed over and returned *in sacculo*, said Aquinas, is not usury.[47] References to a "sealed bag" in this connection are to be found in Olivi and in Bernardino of Siena.[48] In other words, money may be fruitful in the bag, but money out of the bag, in regular circulation, is always barren.

Nevertheless, the scholastics occasionally used the reference in *Eiciens* to idle money to prove that all fruit is due to industry, an inference which does not follow. Thus Antonino of Florence states that he who receives a loan profits from his own industry, because money yields no profit of itself, as can be seen from keeping it in a box (*ut patet tenendo in capsa*).[49] (Customs change while ideas remain the same: the bag, lost in transmission from the ancient source, has reappeared in the shape of a box.) However, Antonino again is only borrowing. One of his frequent sources was Lorenzo Ridolfi, in whom an even more explicit statement of this particular argument can be found. Lorenzo writes: "But money has no utility at all if kept in a box (*arca*), and its use is for exchange, as was said above. And therefore the principal cause of its utility is human industry".[50]

But this is a *non sequitur*. I certainly confess what even a child can see, said Calvin, namely that money would be sterile if

[46] See above, p.74.
[47] *De malo*,XIII,4, p.376.
[48] Olivi, Siena BC U.V.6, f.303va; Bernardino, Sermo 36,3,6, p.216. Olivi poses the example of someone who borrows money *in saccis sigillatam* in order that those who visit him may think him wealthy and therefore honour or fear him more, or in order to avoid some peril or harm by the mere presentation of the money. Bernardino copies.
[49] Antonino, *Summa*,II,i,6,1, col.77.
[50] Ridolfi, loc.cit.

you shut it up in a box (*coffre*).[51] The kind of economic deontology which Max Weber wanted us to associate particularly with the Calvinists, as far as it relates to money, was precisely concerned with the duty of *getting it out of the box*, because it is barren when idle. Put it to work! Put human ingenuity to work on it! This is the "spirit of capitalism" which, according to Weber, comes to expression "in almost classical purity"[52] in Benjamin Franklin's *Advice to a Young Tradesman*: "Remember, that *time* is money". "Remember, that money . . . can beget money, and its offspring can beget more". This, if you please, is a "frontal attack" on scholastic doctrine. But Franklin also stresses the importance of industry: "The way to wealth . . . depends chiefly on two words, *industry* and *frugality*; that is, waste neither *time* nor *money*, but make the best use of both".[53] It is a sin to be idle, but it is likewise a sin to let money lie idle. Money is barren in the box, but human industry fructifies it, and it is right that that which can bear fruit is placed in such circumstances that germination can take place.

This is not the place to rectify the historical slant which certain German sociologists have given to Anglo-Saxon business morality. I have passed briefly over familiar ground just to indicate what must be the obvious retort to the kind of proof of the exclusive fruitfulness of industry proffered by Ridolfi through Antonino. If money is sterile when idle so is human industry of the kind we call entrepreneurship sterile without access to money. This is the position naturally adopted by the advocates of a "moderate" usury doctrine in the age of the break-through of the new economics. Says Zech, Jesuit professor at Ingolstadt in the mid-eighteenth century: "Sterile would often the labours of one man be unless irrigated by the money of another; sterile money unless fecundated by another's industry".[54] Man and money, both languishing in sterility, yearn for

[51] Calvin, *De usuris*, in *Corpus Reformatorum* (CR) 38, col.247.
[52] Weber 48.
[53] *The Works of Benjamin Franklin*, ed. J.Sparks, Vol.II, Boston 1836, p.87, 89.
[54] F.X.Zech, *Rigor moderatus doctrinae pontificiae circa usuras*,II,II,86; in *Theologiae cursus completus*, ed. Migne, Vol.16, Paris 1841, col.905. I traced these quotations through Funk (1), who often appealed to Zech as spokesman for the rearguard defenders of scholastic doctrine.

the fruitful coupling. The capitalist, by whose intervention "the industrious can be furnished with tools",[55] becomes the respectable procurer whose services draw their well-earned compensation.

The common gain belongs *pro rata* to him who joins money with another's industry, suggests Zech.[56] *Pro rata* sounds like an echo of Aristotle. But that is not how things work out in economics. What we have here is a problem of imputation which does not submit to any logical solution along those lines. If there is a potency for fructification in money and in industry, there is no way of allocating shares in the fruit except by recourse to the forces of the market. If human industry can draw a price in the open market, that is how much its contribution is worth. There is nothing to justify a different treatment in the case of money. No one would think of demanding of the entrepreneur that he prove intention not to remain idle if the loan had been denied. By the same token, why should proof of the intention of using his own money be demanded of the capitalist in case he chose not to lend?

This symmetry in the treatment of money and industry signals the abandonment of the sterility dogma, however much Zech and some contemporary moralists may have pretended to maintain it formally. This symmetry was never reached by the pre-Reformation economists, readily though some of their remarks can be construed as tending in this direction. The fact that posterity can question the significance of some of these remarks is evidence of the precariousness of the scholastic position. Once one admits that money is necesssary for industry to fructify, there is no logical way to maintain the asymmetry. One might say that the scholastic economists considered industry the only argument in the production function and money merely a condition defining its area of existence, but this is not even mathematically a meaningful difference from admitting two arguments within the function. In concluding this chapter, then, the legal traditions cannot be said to have provided a

[55] Smith, *Wealth of Nations*,II,4, London 1776, Vol.I, p.427.
[56] Zech, loc. and ed.cit.,§25, col.888.

convincing argument to show why money must be denied a share in the fruits of capitalistic enterprise. The barren metal dogma gleaned from Aristotle's *Politics* must fail as well. Both lines of tradition ran on for centuries. But when Bernardino of Siena and some of the other late scholastics kept insisting that usury is sinful because money is sterile, they could also draw on yet a third tradition, which perhaps stated a more meaningful economic proposition.

6. Money and time

The statement most favoured by those who want to demonstrate Bernardino of Siena's understanding and tolerance of the capitalistic process, is not among the statements quoted in the preceding chapter. It does not even invoke industry as an agent fructifying money but seems to state outright that money has a seminal potential of its own. This is also a long verbatim borrowing from Peter Olivi, broken by a modifying passage (usually not quoted) recalling Gerardo of Siena, and appearing in a sermon where some of the most important terms of analysis had been quoted a few pages earlier, from Gerald Odonis. We have to make our peace now with that famous statement and let it provide an opening for us into the positive usury doctrine of Bernardino's main sources.

The sermon to which I refer is only the third of the Saint's fourteen sermons (Nos. 32-45) devoted to economic subjects. It is preceded by two opening sermons on the conditions of property and exchange in general and is followed immediately by the sermon on pricing where Bernardino publicized the Olivian value analysis. Only then does he turn to usury which is to occupy most of the rest of the series. Sermon 34 is thus also general; the principles set down there apply to all kinds of exchange. It is called *De temporis venditione* and deals with problems of just equivalence in contracts involving a time element.

As indicated in Chapter 4,[1] the early scholastics found an injunction against "selling time" in pseudo-Chrysostom as represented in the *Decretum*, where the anonymous author curses

[1] See above, p.72.

the usurer for selling "a thing not bought but given by God", viz. time. Thus William of Auxerre states that the usurer acts contrary to natural law, for he "sells time, which is common to all creatures".[2] Similarly, Bonaventura: If you acquire something by your industry from a loan and I take part of it back, then "I sell time, which is common and which is not to be sold".[3] Throughout the following centuries, vulgar preachers against usury excelled in lurid descriptions of the punishments befalling those who sold this dimension in which God's children are permitted briefly to live together. Nor is there any shortage of serious authors, from Scotus to Biel, who employ this figure of speech.[4]

However, as an argument it is subject to a familiar objection. This objection may have been first applied to it by Giles of Rome in one of his *quodlibeta*. Citing the injunction against selling what is common to all temporal creatures, Giles points out that exactly the same thing can be done without sin in other objects. Suppose somebody hands over ten horses on the condition that he gets them back together with two more in a year. This is not usury, but clearly it involves "selling time" just as much as usury in money does.[5] Gerardo of Siena was a confrère and disciple of Giles of Rome and took some of his economics from him. This is a case in point. In Gerardo's treatise, the argument about selling time is said to be empty (*frivolus*), "since there are many licit contracts which involve an extension of time".[6] I cannot find that Bernardino of Siena repeated this but it became well known to the late scholastics through Andreae.[7] Writing at about the same time as Gerardo of Siena, Francis of Meyronnes also rejected the argument briefly: "The same can be said about leasing a house for a year".[8]

[2] *Summa*,III,21, f.225va.
[3] *Collationes de decem praeceptis*,VI,19, p.528.
[4] Scotus, *Sent.*IV,15,2, p.325; Buridan, *Comm.Pol.*, Q.I,12, f.17rb, 19ra; Hassia, f.195va; Antonino, col.76; Biel, *Sent.*IV,15,11, f.QQ_1 ra.
[5] *Quodl.*V,24, f.75va.
[6] P.176.
[7] *Mercuriales*, f.161vb.
[8] *Sent.*VI,16,3, f.204ra.

So we are back among houses and horses. The counter-examples provided by Giles of Rome and Francis of Meyronnes are the classical representatives of the contract of *locatio*. These objects can be leased at a profit for a period of time. They are at the owner's risk and the leaseholder must pay a premium; they may deteriorate in use and he must pay for the depletion; they may fructify and he must pay for the fruit. What he pays for is not *time* but what happens to these objects *in time*. The distinction is clear in principle and several centrally placed usury theorists explained it. Best known is the explanation of Giles of Lessines, which has reached modern scholars in Aquinas's *Opera*. Time, says Giles, is God's and given to all in common. But values may change with time for various reasons, viz. by changes in supply, by local differences in demand, as well as by natural increment such as is evident in the case of woods and animals. To charge more according to temporal variations of these kinds is not usury (though it may sometimes be prohibited under different headings). Later on, while referring to Aristotle's condemnation of *tokos* which is breeding money of money, Giles proceeds to make this the basis of a crucial distinction regarding the time element in contracts. For goods on which the passage of time confers an added value there can be charged a higher price when time intervenes, without this being usury; but when this condition is not fulfilled, and time is merely an *extrinsic measure of duration*, then charging more because of the passage of time is usurious practice.[9]

In the version of this explanation which Bernardino of Siena used, the principle is also brought to bear on the proposition that time is common to all and therefore non-vendible. A distinction is made between time which is common and time which is properly that of a given person and vendible by him. Bernardino's version goes back to Olivi and he used it in discussing a case posed by Olivi, but the fifteenth-century preacher evidently prefers the elucidation of the underlying principle which is to be found in Gerald Odonis's paraphrase of

[9] P.421, pp.425-6.

Olivi, and this he inserts in his direct borrowing from the original source. Odonis's elucidation is very similar to that of Giles of Lessines. The injunction against selling time applies only to time in an abstract, metaphysical sense (time as "duration following the first movement"), not to time as duration related to things; time in this second sense is conceded to the performance of someone's work and thus is time belonging to him and vendible by him.[10]

This comes close to invoking *industria*, as can also be seen from its application to the case Bernardino repeats after Olivi. The case involves a lender who is prepared to anticipate the date of repayment of a loan. Olivi argues that since the time remaining of the stipulated loan period is time properly belonging to the borrower (for him to exercise his industry in – as is now stated explicitly), he is free to bargain with the lender about a reduction in the sum to be repaid.[11] Bernardino accepted this solution.[12] Antonino of Florence demurred and claimed the support of Thomas Aquinas.[13] But Aquinas was by then a little passé on the question of *lucrum cessans,* which is clearly what is involved here.

One might perhaps expect the principle applied here to be capable of being extended to the original lending situation. A potential lender might claim that the time for which he is prepared to forgo a certain sum of money is time "conceded to the performance of his work" in connection with this sum of money and that it is therefore properly his own time, which he can sell. If prospects of such profitable performance can be shown to exist (in other words, if *lucrum cessans* can be established), there ought to be no objection to arguing like that. It is true that it would nullify the concept of selling time in connection with usury. Perhaps for this reason, Olivi (and Bernardino following him) makes an about-turn and says that the principle does not apply to the original lender, since the

10 F.96r.

11 *Tertium dubium*, f.305rb-vb.

12 Sermo 34,1,1, pp.165-6.

13 *Summa*,II,i,8,13, col.136.

time in question is conceded to the borrower. This is certainly inconsistent, not necessarily in terms of the practical solution of cases, but at least in terms of the application of principle. Different principles have to be used to nail down different cases where one principle might do.

Noonan devotes considerable attention to Bernardino's admission that time can sometimes be sold, which he considers the worst "blunder in the whole scholastic tradition of usury", asserting that "no one else will ever be found who will say that 'one's own time' can be sold".[14] If one looks a little more closely into the late sources, one will find that the case of the anticipating debtor selling back his own time, often reappears.[15] It is presumably always transmitted through Bernardino of Siena, and since Bernardino quoted Odonis but not Olivi, it is to the former that it is always ascribed, though he supplies only the general principle and not the case to which it is applied. It is my belief that Odonis, always on the lookout for the lender's interests, would have applied his own principle more consistently. So much for "selling time". What it all amounts to, beside the preaching, is that no one is to be allowed to profit *just because time passes.*

It is on this note that we can best approach the place where Bernardino is alleged to have maintained that there is a growth potential in money. The statement in question is to be found in the next-but-one chapter of the same sermon[16] and is taken from another of Olivi's *dubia.*[17] The case involves the owner of a quantity of corn (*bladum*) which he plans to sell at a certain future date when the price is expected to be higher. Agreeing to sell now, it is concluded that he can charge the future price, for two reasons: first, because he must be allowed to keep himself indemnified; second, because "that which in the firm intention of its owner is ordained at some probable profit, has not only the simple character of money or thing, but above that a sort of

14 Noonan 76.

15 Cf., for instance, Platea, f.101v; Ariosto, f.$e_4$ra; Trovamala, f.254rb.

16 Sermo 34,1,3, at p.170.

17 *Sextum dubium*, at f.307ra-b.

seminal character of the profitable, which we commonly call capital" (*quamdam seminalem rationem lucrosi, quam communiter capitale vocamus*). The Latin phrase quoted is identical in the two authors.

Funk unearthed this passage; since then it has become a main key to Bernardino.[18] In the heat of the dispute over the Protestant roots of capitalism, it is understandable that words like these from the pen of a fifteenth-century Tuscan teacher (and a morally strict one at that) could not be left alone, and it is perhaps forgivable that they were sometimes taken a little too far out of context and distorted not a little in transit. While the statement has often been misquoted so as to seem to refer to a money loan, it is clear from the context that the object to which the passage about "a sort of seminal character" alludes in this instance is not money at all but a commodity, and that this commodity is to be sold not lent.

The solution to the case, not even very bold at the time of Olivi, is quite unexceptionable when Bernardino copies it. When merchants move commodities from areas of plenty to areas of scarcity where, by the common estimate of the market, they fetch a higher price, it is clear that they do society a service, for which the higher price, covering transport and other costs (as well as – as some authors, including Olivi, were beginning to realize – providing incentive) is a just remuneration. If such a merchant, on the eve of his departure, is approached by a potential buyer in his own location, it is equally clear that he can charge the price current at the destination of his journey (if the buyer is willing to pay it), deducting for saved expenses. This follows from the principle of indemnity (which may embrace considerations of forgone gain) as set down in the "double rule" of just pricing.[19] The condition is, to quote Olivi *apud* Bernardino, that the commodity sold "in the firm intention of its owner is ordained at some probable profit". By strict analogy, a merchant planning to store a commodity until com-

[18] Funk (2), 149; cf. Brants 134-5, Cossa 150, Rambaud 41, Sombart 320, O'Brien 181, De Roover 29, Gordon 198.

[19] See above, p.47.

mon scarcity causes its price to increase, can charge the future price if asked to sell now. Storage over time is also a public service of merchants; the transition in time is not in principle different from the transition in space. It is not because of the transition that a higher price is charged, but because material conditions change in time and space. To coin a phrase: the merchant is not "selling time". Bernardino in fact breaks off his recitation from Olivi to point this out explicitly: "In this way, properly speaking, more is not paid because of time (*propter tempus*) but because of the nature of the thing, which is worth more at one time than at another".

The "seminal character of the profitable" of which our text speaks is thus to be found in forward-looking commercial activity in general. This is an interesting observation if not surprising in the case of Olivi, who made a number of remarks like that about economics. But it is not an observation denying the sterility of money. The sterility of money is a proposition concerning usury, i.e. concerning money in the money-market, not concerning the purchasing power of money (or the price of any commodity) at different points in time. It is quite inconceivable that Olivi or Bernardino would have risked misunderstanding by making the remark quoted above in the context of a case of usury. As Bernardino explained it in a later sermon, sterility can also apply to other commodities than money, such as for instance corn, but only when they are objects of a *mutuum*. If by *bladum* these authors had meant *standing corn*, the owner could legitimately compute a price differential because of value increase with time if the field of corn were to be leased; but since by *bladum* they undoubtedly here mean *harvested corn*, i.e. *grain*, which is a fungible, no price differential can be computed in a contract of *mutuum*. This is an extremely important distinction. It goes to the very heart of late scholastic usury theory. The clinching argument of that theory rested on the proposition that money, like any fungible, must be considered as having a fixed and immutable value over time. It is clear that commodity values change, and that the general purchasing power of money changes. One reason for this is individual need, which the scholastics rejected as a just price determinant. Another reason is common need, which they accepted in that connection. But in connection with loan contracts, both are equally irrelevant.

Bernardino inherited this teaching both from Peter Olivi and from Gerardo of Siena. In both these earlier authors it constitutes their first natural law argument against usury. Bernardino copies Gerardo for his own first argument and much further on copies Olivi for his ninth argument.[20] Noticing the evident similarity, he refers back from the ninth to the first argument: there is a lot of repetition like this in the patchwork which is Bernardino on usury. The compiler must also have known Odonis's objection to Olivi's first argument. This objection, which anticipates those of Summenhart and the moderns, is ignored by Bernardino. To complete the picture of the interrelationships between these authors, it seems clear that Gerardo builds on Olivi here. In his version, the brief first argument is only one among many. In Gerardo's adaptation, it is made to carry the burden of the ensuing arguments as well. This first argument maintains its decisive role both in Bernardino's treatise and in Joannes Andreae's annotated edition of Gerardo in the *Quaestiones mercuriales*.[21] Invoking Olivi as we need him, it is therefore proper that we now devote our attention fully to Gerardo of Siena's natural law case against usury, which stands at the very centre of the late scholastic tradition.

Gerardo proceeds in two steps, first rejecting or setting aside for "correction", five traditional arguments, then posing four arguments of his own.[22] In connection with Aristotelian usury doctrine I quoted his objection to the simple, "biological" sterility argument.[23] We have now just seen how he rejected the argument about "selling time", following Giles of Rome. Like Giles, he also turned down the argument about the non-

[20] Sermo 38,1,1 and 9, pp.242-3, p.252.

[21] Op.cit., ff.161vb-162ra. Passing through either Andreae or Bernardino (or both), versions of Gerardo of Siena's positive arguments against usury reappear in a number of later authors, such as Ridolfi, f.16rb-va; Antonino, coll.76-7; Roselli, f.70ra-b; Ariosto, f.a$_3$ra-b, to mention only some who wrote before 1500. They are also important as serving to formalize the definite scholastic position soon to be attacked by Summenhart and his followers.

[22] Pp.174-6, 176-182.

[23] See above, p.61.

deterioration of money.[24] Among the other canon law arguments, the one about the transfer of ownership and the main Thomist argument improving on it, were not rejected out of hand but rather corrected in the light of his own positive arguments.[25] Gerardo's second and third arguments, both building on the first, serve for this purpose, as we shall see presently. Then follows the fourth and final argument, which is the finalistic argument from Aristotle, already quoted, and most likely again inspired by Giles of Rome.[26]

His first and fundamental argument Gerardo bases on the proposition that any fungible is always of equal value to itself. In this he builds on Olivi. Nothing is worth more than itself, says Olivi in the corresponding argument. Since non-fungibles change in themselves, therefore also their values change, but in a fungible, which does not change, just equality is established if a pint is returned for a pint.[27] In a natural fungible, says Gerardo of Siena, value is completely determined either by weight (as in the case of gold or silver) or by measure (as in the case of grain, wine or oil). Similarly, in an artificial fungible like money, value is determined by number. Usury, therefore, (in a favoured phrase) consists in causing a natural thing to be valued above its nature or (as in the case of money) in causing "an artificial thing to be valued above and beyond the artifice it embodies" (*rem artificialem suae arti supervalere*).

Since we are mainly concerned with money (where physical equality *can* be established by a simple count), let us grant these authors a minor point and just mention it because it leads to a graver problem. To return a bottle of *ordinaire* for a bottle of *Château Margaux* is not fair exchange; they are not in any relevant sense equal measures of the fungible wine. There is clearly a quality clause involved, but quality in wine is a matter of taste and quality in most fungibles partly a matter of judgment. Thus, even if the fungible were to be broken down into

[24] See p.74 and note 8 to Chapter 4.
[25] See above, p.81 and pp.89-90.
[26] See above, pp.68-69 and cf. p.66.
[27] F.301va.

countless subspecies, there might be problems involved in reaching agreement as to equivalence.

This kind of problem would be avoided if the principle were to be limited to the fungible money, but it is essential that it should hold for all fungibles, not only as regards its validity in the usury discussion, but as regards its significance when applied to money. The main objection to the proposition does not concern the evaluation of possibly different items of some broad species of fungible at a given point in time but rather the evaluation of exactly identical items of a given fungible (for instance money) at different points in time. No object is evaluated in isolation but in relation to other objects and to circumstances prevailing in the context of judgment. Tastes may change, and need and scarcity may intervene to influence value relations.

Gerardo of Siena was aware of this. However, he says, if such objects "sometimes seem to increase or decrease, this is not on account of any increase or decrease in the value which inheres in them but on account of increase or decrease in our demand or also on account of increase or decrease in the value of other things for which they are exchanged". In economics, as we conceive of it, such circumstantial changes are what *determine* value. This is precisely Gerald Odonis's objection to Olivi's first argument. There does exist an absolute substantial value in objects determined by their rank in the natural order of creation, says Odonis, citing St Augustine, but what counts in economic exchange is the value of objects in human use.[28] This was a distinction pointed out by Aquinas, Scotus and others and used by Odonis also in his discussion of exchange in the *Ethics* commentary.[29] But to Olivi and Gerardo of Siena when discussing usury this kind of comparison does not count. What counts is only intrinsic value.

However (and this is most important), intrinsic value is not used to compare objects with each other, only to compare an object with itself. If the principle described above were to be

[28] F.91r.

[29] Ed. Brescia 1482, f.X_4vb; cf. Langholm (1) 87-8.

limited to money, we might be back in the kind of usury theory attributed by some critics to Thomas Aquinas on account of his statement in the *Sentences* commentary that usury amounts to diversifying the money measure.[30] The way this has been read is that there exists one fixed and immutable value measure in economics, namely the legal face value of money. Other values may change but not the value of money. In money loans this would coincide with Gerardo's principle, but not in other loans. The way Aquinas has been (wrongly) interpreted, the loan of a bushel of wheat would have to be repaid with more or less than a bushel of wheat of the same quality depending on variations in the value of wheat relative to money.

Extending the principle to all fungibles clearly implies (in Keynesian terms) that all fungibles have simultaneous zero own-rates of interest. But the scholastics were hardly aware of the implications for capital theory of a condition like that. All they sought to do was eliminate resort in the case of any fungible to some immutable standard of comparison outside that fungible itself. As far as usury was concerned, there simply did not exist any standard of value of the kind which economists were to pursue in vain some centuries later: not corn, nor labour, nor utility, individual or aggregate, are relevant to the exchange of wine for wine. In exchange for itself, wine is autonomous: it is the measure of its own value. So are all natural fungibles. So is money. Money is nothing special. It is not that its value is given where other values change. Gerardo of Siena does not express any particular idea about the nature of money as a measure, any more than Aquinas did. The purchasing power of money may rise and fall, just as the values of other objects may rise and fall. It is just that this is irrelevant when money is lent and repaid in money. Then money is a measure of its own value. A piece of coin is a piece of coin.

Gerardo says about money that "art, in its way, prescribed to moneys, being artificially invented, a value by their count". It is presumably possible to construe this statement so as to embody

[30] See above, p.83.

a "sign theory" of money, according to which the value of money is nominal value as stipulated by the coiner and announced by the mark stamped upon the coin. A piece of coin of given face value would then be worth another piece of coin of the same face value or a third of a piece of triple face value. But it is interesting to ask how debasement would be viewed on Gerardo's premises and whether the physical properties of a coin as expressed by its precious metal content would not be the bearing principle. The question is not raised. The fact that the author expressly distinguishes between gold and silver as natural fungibles and money as an artificial fungible cannot be taken automatically to mean that natural properties are overruled by legal decree.

If a basis for the self-valuation principle is to be sought in Aristotle, it is difficult to avoid an association with the *Metaphysics*. According to Aristotle's theory of measurement as propounded in that work, any object is measured by the smallest unit of its kind.[31] Thus corn measures corn and wine measures wine. In the exchange of different objects for one another, this kind of measurement is inapplicable. Yet equivalence must be established in some way; some other kind of measure is required. Discussing justice in exchange in commentary on Aristotle's *Ethics*, a number of scholastics of the tradition to which Gerald Odonis belonged, while acknowledging the metaphysical measure as correct *per se*, found a measure *per accidens* in human need. Different commodities have different values according to human estimation, and on that basis, just barter relations can be established. Money is also subject to human valuation, and just prices can thus be established in indirect (monetary) exchange.[32] Should we glance back at the case of future exchange posed by Olivi and Bernardino,[33] this is the valuation principle which applies. But when money is actually exchanged for money, or corn for corn, or wine for wine, as in a *mutuum*, then no such accidental measure is

[31] *Metaphysics*,X, 1052b-1053a.
[32] See Langholm (1), mainly Chapter 3.
[33] See above, pp.115-17.

needed; each thing provides it own measure. There is no call to go beyond first principles. In the Middle Ages, economics was not yet an autonomous science, safe in its own truths. Truth must be sought on other grounds, and the safest ground was metaphysics.

Nevertheless, to brush off the principle of the self-valuation of fungibles as an intrusion of metaphysics into a domain where it does not belong, would be unfortunate if it obscured the force of a proper economic argument established on the basis of the principle. It is wise to recall that normative economics cannot do without extraneous premises of one kind or another. To assume that purchasing power concedes a right, as modern economics implicitly does, is as questionable an ethical premise as to assume that purchasing power is a constant to be ignored, as in effect the scholastics did ignore it. It may be objected that if one wants to explain why usury is wrong, it is useful to be able to explain why it is actually being paid, and this explanation may suffer by the self-valuation principle. This objection may be partly countered by reference to the obvious truth that explanations of facts based on certain moral and institutional premises now accepted are of only secondary interest to a theory which ignores or questions those premises. If changes in purchasing power serve to explain the fact and rate of interest, it is because these phenomena are permitted to establish themselves. According to the scholastic vision of society there is no good reason why there should normally exist such changes, and if they occasionally occur, there may be good reason to arrest them. This is to be a main clue to the final assessment of scholastic usury doctrine in our concluding chapter and further discussion of it may be postponed for a few pages. It may be added here that most changes in value relations of the kinds ruled out by Gerardo of Siena are of course irrelevant to usury theory anyhow and just confuse the picture. After all, we do not primarily pay interest on a loan of corn because corn prices change or interest on money because the general price level changes. Contemporary theorists will testify to some tricky relationships on this point, but all will seek elsewhere for the fundamental explanation of interest. Unfortunately, some of those who have criticized the scholastic doctrine have not been economists and have confused interest and price indexing.

From the self-valuation of fungibles there follows the *sterility of fungibles*. This is Gerardo of Siena's second argument against usury:

> To loanable things, in which usury is committed, there is prescribed from nature or from art a determined value, and consequently they cannot increase in value and for the same reason cannot generate any fruit, since a thing which generates a fruit will always increase in value with the fruit, for it is of greater value when in fruit than when it is without fruit. Since therefore a usurious contract makes something which is of determined value and therefore fruitless increase in value and thus produce a profit, it follows that that which cannot fructify is made profitable, which is entirely unnatural and vicious.

Joannes Andreae, Bernardino of Siena and other users of Gerardo quoted this passage. This is what sterility came to mean to the late scholastics who had rejected the "barren metal" dogma originally read into Aristotle's *Politics*. Sterility applies to all fungibles, natural and artificial, and does not pertain to any specific physical or biological properties of such objects except indirectly, in that the property of fungibility determines the way these objects must be evaluated. Gerardo used his second argument to "correct" the old canon law argument from ownership. His third argument, which restates and thus "corrects" the Thomist consumptibility argument in terms of value, is derived in much the same way: A thing having always a given value cannot increase in value with use; use and substance are one value and the sum must remain constant.

While adopting the mature teleological position derived from Aristotle as his main frame of reference, Gerardo of Siena thus in fact draws all the relevant inherited arguments together within this frame in a sterility argument which owes to Aristotle nothing but its name. The legal argument from ownership and the consumptibility argument of Aquinas, as well as in effect what might remain of the patristic argument about the non-vendibility of time, all remain valid only in so far as they may be restated as secondary formulations of the basic principle that fungibles are immutable in value with time and in that sense barren. In concluding this chapter it may be useful to summarize Gerardo's premises and state this final scholastic position on sterility in terms which indicate the point in which it was to be attacked by post-scholastic critics.

To this end, consider first some non-fungible (leasable) object like a field, a horse, or a house. For such objects time is not merely an "extrinsic measure of duration", for they may change with time in various ways. They may grow or deteriorate with time and they may yield various kinds of usufruct, either physically or by profitable use. To permit subsequent comparison, assume value relations to other objects to be constant. Growth and deterioration can be taken loosely, but on the whole work against one another. Thus a horse grows in strength and stature in its second year, but deteriorates in the sense that one year takes out of its total life span that much future service potential. Similarly, usufruct works with deterioration against growth. The harder a horse is driven in a given year, the more it deteriorates and the more its growth will be stunted. To work a field harder in order to increase the harvest will exhaust the soil. If a field is still unharvested when its "substance value" is computed at the end of the season, growth is positive and usufruct is zero. If the field is evaluated after harvesting, the increment is reported as usufruct rather than growth. Both must be understood as net values, after deductions for cost and industry. Usufruct (or "use value") may then be negative, as may also growth less deterioration. However, if in some non-fungible the sum of substance value and use value at the end of a certain period exceeds the substance value at the beginning of the period, then the increment is rightly the owner's, and such an object may be leased at a price.

By contrast, consider a fungible like wine, corn – or money. For such an object, time is nothing but an extrinsic measure of duration, for it does not grow or deteriorate but is always equal to itself in physical characteristics as well as in value. Therefore, says Gerardo of Siena as copied by the late scholastics, such an object can have no separate use value. The value of its substance is in fact the same thing as the value of its use, for substance and use are alienated together and consumed together. If usury is paid for the loan of such an object, then (first argument) "it is valued above its nature or artifice", or (second argument) "a fruitless object is made profitable", or (third argument) "of two things which are of one value, one is made to increase with the other". If this were to be allowed, it is as though the fungible, continually in use and continually fructifying, would increase in value endlessly into the future, which is clearly absurd.

There is no question but that this triple argument could hold a certain fascination, and authors in the waning scholastic tradition clung to it for centuries. Today it will immediately be met with the objection that it draws an erroneous comparison. It makes no sense to compare values at different points in time. What must be compared are a present valuation of a present object and a present valuation of a future expectation. When we look into the future, through imaginary time, there is a foreshortening of the perspective. Evaluated today, a certain quantity of a given fungible at one's disposal a year hence is worth less than the same quantity of the same fungible available at once. Hence, while any fruit-bearing object may well remain of the same value when evaluated at consecutive points in real time, in our present expectation its progressively diminishing future value together with its increasing (through also foreshortened) use value, will add up to a constant equal to its actual present value. If this foreshortening of a person's future time perspective equals the rate of interest payable by him when he borrows such an object for a period of time, then he is equally well off.

But why is there such foreshortening of the time perspective in the case of money? Why do we value present money above future money? For centuries after the collapse of scholastic doctrine the answer used to be: because money does bear fruit. It is true that this fruit does not register on money as an object. It is truly barren in that naïve sense. For the sake of argument, it may also be conceded that money not only remains the same physically but that its value at consecutive points in time remains the same. The point then is that this can happen in the case of other fruit-bearing objects as well. Thus a field may be leased in the spring and returned in precisely the same condition next spring, and yet a crop has grown and has been harvested and sold and the proceeds consumed. Even in the case of a horse it must happen at least once near its peak that its substance value at a given date in two consecutive years is precisely the same, "growth" exactly compensating for "deterioration", and yet the possessor of the horse during that year has taken out of it a positive use value. If this kind of thing can happen to other fruit-bearing objects it can and must happen to money, for the very obvious reason that the possessor of money can invest it in such a fruit-bearing object.

One must not forget what happens to money after it has been "consumed" by alienation. Money does not fructify in the shape of money but after a metamorphosis which turns it into real capital. Tell me, said Calvin, when I buy a field, does not money breed money?[34] Or three and a half centuries later, in Alfred Marshall's *Principles of Economics:*

> Aristotle had said that money was barren, and that to derive interest from lending it out was to put it to an unnatural use. And following his lead Scholastic writers argued with much labour and ingenuity that he who lent out a house or a horse might charge for its use, because he gave up the enjoyment of a thing that was directly productive of benefit. But . . . they obscured the fact that he who borrows money can buy, for instance, a young horse, whose services he can use, and which he can sell, when the loan has to be returned, at as good a price as he paid for him.[35]

But as an objection to scholastic doctrine, this is partly beside the point. If the owner of a horse can lend it and get it back unimpaired and with a profit in a year, it is not immediately

[34] CR 38, 247.
[35] Marshall 585.

obvious that he must forgo all of this profit if he sells it now. Future profit will be anticipated in the present market estimation of the horse, less the market rate of interest. If the rate of interest is zero, the whole future profit on the horse will be anticipated in its present price. He who borrows money in order to buy such a horse and sell it again in a year, while paying no interest on the money loan, will make no profit on the horse deal either. He will be compensated for his cost and "industry" by deductions from the gross use value of the horse, but will receive no surplus attributable to money as such. If the market rate of interest is positive, he will make enough to pay this rate of interest. The fact that he has held cash briefly gives him no advantage beyond the opportunity to exercise his industry while in possession of the horse. Under the latter assumption it is clearly unreasonable that our particular borrower and prospective horse-buyer should be exempt from interest and pocket the profit himself. But Marshall's argument does not explain why everybody should pay interest, and what the scholastics said is that nobody should.

7. The need to borrow

When the theory of interest dropped out of the Schools (so to speak), it embarked on a circuitous journey which has only recently brought it back to face in earnest the teaching it rejected. Minutely recording the successive legs of that journey, Böhm-Bawerk in the first volume of his monumental study of capital theory demonstrated convincingly that the kind of fructification and productivity arguments favoured by almost all economists from Calvin to Marshall are in fact invalid on the premises conventionally prepared for them. Specific postulates either about external economic circumstances or about human mentality or both have to be introduced in order to prove that present money is worth more than present expectation of future money and thus to show why interest is paid on money loans. As we all know, Böhm-Bawerk in his second volume worked his patient way to formulating three such assumptions, and from these, often in opposition to their originator, two lines of modern interest theory have developed.[1]

One line, which may perhaps be called the psychological line of interest theory, is associated with Böhm-Bawerk's first and second "Gründe" and among subsequent writers primarily with the American economist Irving Fisher – to the latter's regret, since he kept insisting quite justifiably that he had not neglected the third "Grund". However, it was that third reason alleged by Böhm-Bawerk, according to which interest is derived from the time extension of the capitalistic production process, which the main line of modern interest theory took as its point of departure. Being normally conceived of as an integral part of capital

[1] Böhm-Bawerk,II, Book III,iii, "Gegenwart und Zukunft in der Wirtschaft", pp.248-299.

theory, this line branched off into the various systems of Wicksell, Schumpeter, and Hayek, not to mention the partial refinements in mathematical terms subsequently added by numerous contemporary economists. What is common to these efforts is that they study the behaviour of interest as a parameter in models of economic growth.

In recent years a number of papers and books devoted to the memory of Joseph Schumpeter have once again brought to the fore the provocative proposition underlying the Schumpeterian version of growth theory, namely that Böhm-Bawerk's "third reason" vanishes, and interest with it, in the "circular flow" of a completely stationary economy, unless occasional disturbances and irregularities in the minds and circumstances of individuals force them to borrow.[2] What they pay then *is* interest in a sense but not true interest in the Schumpeterian sense and thus of less account to those who primarily want to know what happens when economies take off into sustained growth. To students of growth theory, Schumpeter's zero interest proposition defines a limiting state, never attained in real life but fascinating the way such limiting states are for the paradoxes and contradictions they sometimes embody. The present author can claim but modest competence to judge the validity of the various statements of modern growth theory. What seems to be the consensus now is that Schumpeter cannot be logically shown to be wrong, nor can he be proven unconditionally right. It all depends how factors identified under conditions familiar to us will operate when they are carried to unrealistic extremes.

However, there also seems to be agreement that in a near-stationary economy, much less interest is paid on accounts associated with Böhm-Bawerk's third reason than on accounts associated with his first and second reasons. What I would like to do in this summing up of scholastic usury theory is therefore to use Schumpeter's zero interest model as a take-off point for a different kind of comparison from the one made by modern growth theorists. Instead of analysing positive Schumpeterian

[2] Schumpeter (1).

interest in a growth model against the background of the stationary zero position, I propose to discuss that kind of *non*-Schumpeterian interest which is actually being paid in a stationary economy against the same background. Rather than illuminating the phenomena which cause interest to be legitimately paid under current conditions, I believe this alternative comparison to be the best way to reveal the very different forces at work behind medieval usury practice and to explain why the scholastics condemned it so strongly.

The stationary economy is a fiction. There never was in real life an economy without some growth (or some decay), just as there never was in real life an economy in equilibrium. I want to emphasize this fairly obvious fact clearly lest I be accused of justifying the scholastic usury doctrine on the ground that it was aimed at a non-growth economy where interest ought to be zero for that reason alone. On the other hand I believe that usury doctrine developed in some relationship to the growth rates of the European economies and that the overruling of the Church's prohibition in the sixteenth century and increasingly in the seventeenth and eighteenth centuries must be seen partly as a consequence of a dawning realization of the kind of forces envisaged by growth theorists today. Those forces certainly were at work earlier. Actual growth rates are difficult to estimate in the absence of reliable statistics, but by all accounts the thirteenth and early fourteenth centuries, when our authors theorized and moralized, appear in retrospect as a period of increasing commercial and industrial activity. Entrepreneurs were rearing their heads all over the continent, getting things moving, needing credit. But theorists are usually a little behind their times, and moralists usually a little behind the theorists. While the economies were definitely on the move about them, the high scholastics still possessed a picture of the world in stasis.

When the ancient philosophers pictured the ideal state, it was a state so stationary that they could count to a head the number of its inhabitants. When times moved, it was with the seasons. If you stayed a year, you left exactly where you came. This was the model of the world received by the scholastics from time immemorial, and it was reinforced by Scripture and by Aristotle. In this kind of model, growth interest does not exist. A number of the assumptions recorded in the preceding chapters specify this overall assumption and can be reasonably explained only as expressions of it. When Gerardo of Siena can assume that a sum of money today is an adequate value measure of the same sum of money a year hence, he is in fact assuming fixed tastes, fixed quantities of commodities and of money metal, presumably a fixed population, too – thus ruling out a different kind of modern growth theory. As will be remembered (and as will be commented on again shortly), risk of loss of principal was ruled out by a legal device. What this approaches is not so very different from the Schumpeterian zero interest stationary state. On the scholastic premises, it is not such an unreasonable picture of the world.

Why, then, is anybody willing to pay interest under the limiting conditions imposed by this stationary state? To review some other theoretical features presumably well known to the reader, the main psychological reason is what Fisher called "time preference", i.e. the tendency to underestimate future "psychic income" (what used to be called "pleasures") compared with a present one. As the parenthesis is meant to indicate, but as is now often lost sight of, this principle in British political economy goes back to Jeremy Bentham. Treating of the measurement of pleasures and pains, Bentham makes the strength of such experiences depend on four circumstances, including the "*propinquity* or *remoteness*" of a pleasure (or a pain).[3] The year 1871 saw the publication of two books on economics destined for lasting fame, namely the *Theory* of Jevons and the *Grundsätze* of Menger, both of whom acknowledge this principle, Jevons explicitly invoking Bentham.[4] When Böhm-Bawerk wrote some years later, he acknowledged both forerunners, while Menger in his second edition erased this Böhm-Bawerkian foothold in his own writing, so opposed was

[3] *An Introduction to the Principles of Morals and Legislation*, Chapter IV, ed. W.Harrison, Oxford 1948, p.151.

[4] Jevons 33.

he to his pupil's use of it.[5] In Böhm-Bawerk this constitutes the "second reason". Much of the latter's analysis was also anticipated by John Rae, the mid-nineteenth-century Scottish eclectic. Rae offers a colourful explanation of psychic time preference in the following words.

> The actual presence of the immediate object of desire in the mind, by exciting the attention, seems to rouse all the faculties, as it were, to fix their view on it, and leads them to a very lively conception of the enjoyments which it offers to their instant possession. The prospects of future good, which future years may hold out to us, seem at such a moment dull and dubious, and are apt to be slighted, for objects on which the day-light is falling strongly, and showing us in all their freshness just within our grasp.[6]

Except for Fisher and his school (most notably Fetter), this psychological principle sits loosely and uncomfortably among the premises of almost all later versions of capital theory, for two very understandable reasons. First, because it takes the explanation of economic phenomena straight out of economics and into psychology (if not ethics), leaving little for the professional economist to argue about. Second, because it is virtually impossible in any given instance to extricate these motivational aspects from external economic circumstances. Clearly, time preference not only explains interest; it is also partly to be explained by interest and by other phenomena also correlated with interest.

Böhm-Bawerk was well aware of this and only introduced time preference ("die Unterschätzung künftiger Bedürfnisse") after explaining carefully a conditional circumstance, namely "die Verschiedenheit des Verhältnisses von Bedarf und Deckung", being his "first reason". Pure time preference oper-

[5] In the first edition, Chapter III, §3b, on the productivity of capital, contains a psychologically flavoured paragraph (pp.127-8) obviously serving as a springboard for Böhm-Bawerk. In the posthumous second edition (Vienna 1923) this material is in Chapter IV, §6b (p.97) without the regretted paragraph.

[6] Rae, *Statement of Some New Principles on the Subject of Political Economy*, Boston 1834, p.120.

ates only in comparison between numerically or quantitatively equal incomes (goods, pleasures) in present and future. If future quantities are expected to be larger than present ones, borrowing at interest in order to increase present compared with future quantities need not reflect time preference in this sense but merely a normal scheme of decreasing marginal utility. However, as several writers following Böhm-Bawerk have assumed, a tendency to expect the future to be more plentiful than the present, for real or imagined reasons, is not uncommon. The first and second reasons therefore work together.

They can also be conceived of as working in combination with something reminiscent of Böhm-Bawerk's third reason on the individual level, even if that reason is rejected in the precise technical sense in which the author himself stated it (as it now tends to be, but we need not go into that difficulty here). An expected increased future income may be a reason for anticipating the future and paying something for this temporal redistribution of income, but for any individual in any given situation, future income may be contingent on his borrowing not only in so far as it reduces future income by anticipating it but in so far as it increases it owing to opportunities opening up through borrowing. This is how the industry/money dichotomy of the scholastics ties on to modern categories and is finally resolved. There is an important sense in which money fructifies industry through what Fisher calls *investment opportunity*. If the individual is short of money his industry is circumscribed or even paralysed. Only by getting his hands on money (and reducing future income by paying interest) can he increase the future income from which interest must be deducted, by reaping the fruits of industry.

All these factors may well operate together in the stationary economy without constituting any payment of interest in the true Schumpeterian sense, representing nothing but shifts in income distribution creating no surplus. It follows from what was said above that they can motivate productive as well as consumptive interest. If the shoemaker's shop burns down and the artisan dies in the fire, his widow may be reduced to borrowing for consumption. If the shop burns but the shoemaker survives, he may borrow both for consumption and in order to rebuild his shop and replace his tools. Both can happen within the circular flow. It is particularly important to emphasize this in view of the fallacy committed by many historians of medieval usury practice and compounded by students of the theory of the stationary economy, that of supposing that loans contracted under such circumstances are mainly loans for consumption. The impression given by systematic study of the scholastic treatises on usury does not confirm the notion that they mainly envisaged such loans. On the contrary, they addressed themselves to situations where the borrower planned to put his loan to productive use by means of his industry as often as to the situation of the impoverished widow who must borrow to eat. That was not to them a crucial distinction, and the crux of their doctrine can be lost sight of if this distinction is focused on too strongly.

In order to approach the consideration truly underlying the scholastics' condemnation of usury on loans of both these kinds, it is necessary to remove another element interfering with the relationship between present and future income, namely risk. When we tend to underestimate future prospects compared with present facts, the reason is frequently that those prospects are risky: a bird in the hand is better than two or more in the bushes of the future. According to De Roover, Bernardino of Siena "recognized at one point that present goods are more valuable than future goods, a principle which, centuries later, was invoked (by Böhm-Bawerk) as the economic justification of interest".[7] I find that observation inaccurate. Böhm-Bawerk explicitly ruled out risk before stating his "three reasons", and what Bernardino speaks of in the passage referred to is risk. Incidentally, it is not Bernardino who speaks but (as usual) Olivi copied by Bernardino.[8] Possession of a thing in the present is more valuable than a future right of possession, says Olivi, for present certainty is greater and more valuable than future cer-

[7] De Roover 30.

[8] Olivi, f.306va; cf. Bernardino, Sermo 34,1,2, p.167.

tainty. I admit that this comparison of two "certainties" is ambiguous in the original, but Bernardino's rendering ought to leave no doubt as to what is meant, for he again employs the device of breaking into the recitation from Olivi with an explanatory note, stating that possession is safer (*securius*) than a mere right of possession. So it is still an open question whether pure time preference can be located in a scholastic author. I have found little solid evidence of it, though they had a clear invitation in Aristotle, as we shall see presently. But they knew about risk.

The way the scholastics generally treated of risk in connection with usury was discussed briefly in Chapter 4.[9] It is open to serious objection. Risk is usually ruled out by a legal technicality which focuses on the just terms of contract, assuming that these terms will be fulfilled, and according to a contract of *mutuum*, repayment is due even if the principal is lost, since ownership passes to the borrower. It is obvious that medieval rates of interest were often materially higher because of risk of failure of repayment, in spite of the terms of contract and despite whatever security and collateral might be raised. However, as was also pointed out when this was discussed before, the scholastics strongly condemned usury for reasons applying to money loans even when this kind of risk is absent, and it is these reasons that can be illuminated by comparison with modern capital theory which also, for purposes of exposition, frequently disregards risk. I am not saying that this exonerates scholastic usury doctrine as far as risk is concerned (any more than it validates contemporary theory "under certainty"), but it permits us to get on the right track towards understanding what the doctrine was really about, and what it was not about was risk.

Thus (somewhat high-handedly) bypassing risk, we can approach the essence of usury doctrine by another long stride if we consider for a moment the kind of market (or rather the lack of markets) in which loan transactions are concluded in the

[9] See above, pp.78-80.

near-stationary economy. Henri Pirenne lent his great authority to the summary proposition that there did not truly exist such a thing as a market for money in Europe in the Middle Ages.[10] Institutional details cannot be entered into here. Instances of banking activity contradict the generalization, and they multiplied rapidly in the course of the period under observation here. This does not alter the fact that the general absence or rudimentary state of money markets in the centuries in which the scholastic doctrine took form, provides an extremely important clue to the doctrine.

In the absence of the credit institutions by which growth is financed, money circulates as a medium of exchange and is available for purposes of lending and borrowing only accidentally and erratically. He who has money to lend is often a monopolist facing a borrower with little choice among alternative lenders. If a perfect money market could be envisaged in a coin economy of this kind, coins flowing freely among those willing to borrow and those willing to lend, competition would necessarily bring the rate of interest far below what was actually paid in the Middle Ages, even discounting for risk and transaction costs. It would be a market rate determined only by the equalized time preferences, adjusted for future income expectations and investment opportunities, of the marginal potential borrower and lender. If the rate could remain so high, it was largely because these marginal agents seldom met. As in the case of commodity exchange, but to a much larger extent, the exchangers of money met away from contact with operative, competitive markets ensuring a just common estimate of value.

If money markets had existed, would this just common market estimate of the value of the use of money tend towards a zero level? "Within the circular flow", says Schumpeter, "and in a market which is in equilibrium it is impossible with a given money sum to obtain a greater money sum".[11] This is, in Schumpeterian terms, a statement of the sterility of money in a stationary economy. Implicitly it is what the scholastics taught.

[10] Pirenne 139.
[11] Schumpeter (1) 189.

It explains why the market criterion was not activated in the case of money-lending as it was in the case of commodity exchange, thus reducing usury teaching mostly to a discussion of indemnity under extrinsic titles. For the purpose of exploring the logic of a hypothetical system, the theorist is entitled to make a wide range of analytical assumptions. The scholastics, however, were offering moral advice to practitioners, and this puts their assumptions to a stricter test of validity. Apart from the question of the rate of interest in the stationary economy, no economy was, as I said, completely stationary. In the economies to which the scholastics addressed themselves, some positive rate of interest would certainly have established itself under free market competition, if such a state of affairs could be imagined. The grounds implicitly relied on by the scholastics for condemning all usury therefore involve a simplification, and their moral advice was bound to suffer to the extent that this simplification distorted empirical facts. Nevertheless, it served to arrest all manifestations of another factor which on the overall moral premises of the scholastics was unquestionably a greater evil, namely the exploitation by the resourceful lender of the resourceless borrower unprotected by the justice of the market.

If the scholastics had seen fit to follow an invitation by Aristotle in his psychological work, they might have demonstrated the position of the medieval borrower in a way which points up very clearly the analogy with commodity exchange. However, they let this opportunity pass, and we shall have to turn to Böhm-Bawerk and the sources and critics of his interest theory in order to make this point. It may surprise the economist familiar with the concept of time preference but less so with Greek philosophy to learn that this is also an Aristotelian concept. Aristotle's *De anima* was translated by William of Moerbeke and commented on by Albert the Great and Thomas Aquinas as well as a number of later scholastics including Buridan. However, the context was so far removed from the problem of usury that a most fruitful suggestion potentially relating to usury which Aristotle there makes was lost on them all. In the third book of *De anima* the author rounds off his analysis of the mind by discussing the appetitive principles which govern animal behaviour. In that connection he points out (among other acute observations) that "in creatures which have a sense of time" a particular behavioural conflict may occur, in that "the mind advises us to resist with a view to the future, while desire only looks to the present; for what is momentarily pleasant seems to be absolutely pleasant and absolutely good, because desire cannot look to the future".[12]

This psychological hypothesis, that desire "cannot look to the future" while reason can, provides a partial explanation of time preference for modern exponents of that principle as well. Underestimation of the future in the sense of Böhm-Bawerk's "second reason" (what has come to be called an "intrinsic rate of time preference"[13] to distinguish it from the effects of material economic circumstances and opportunities) is regularly associated with irrationality, with the triumph of desire over reason. John Rae saw it as "passion getting the better of mere prudence";[14] to Jevons it expressed a lack of "good sense and foresight".[15] According to most interpreters, this could have something to do with the state of maturity both in the individual and in the culture to which he belongs. Böhm-Bawerk found it outspoken in "children and savages", a phrase copied both by Schumpeter in his early work and by Fetter.[16] Rae made a point of racial differences with regard to time preference.[17] Schumpeter, discussing Böhm-Bawerk's principles in his *History*, confirmed his view that "individuals, classes, and nations differ greatly in this respect".[18] Fisher (USA, *anno* 1930) found thoughtless neglect of the future more characteristic of negroes than of whites.[19] Since lender and borrower in medieval Europe were systematically different as to race, these observations open

[12] 433b; W.S.Hett's translation; Loeb Classical Library, No.288.
[13] Samuelson 61.
[14] Rae 121.
[15] Jevons 75-6.
[16] Böhm-Bawerk II, 266; cf. Schumpeter (1) 35, Fetter 240.
[17] Rae, Chapter VII; ed.cit., pp.130-163.
[18] Schumpeter (2) 929.
[19] Fisher 375.

"contempt for the bleeding of the necessitous and the exploiting of the thoughtless or profligate".[23]

Nowhere are these factors more graphically demonstrated than in a table constructed by Irving Fisher in order to suggest some numerical magnitudes of time preference in persons of different character and in different circumstances, as reproduced below.[24]

	Time-preference of different individuals with different incomes Individuals who are		
	shortsighted, weak willed, accustomed to spend, without heirs	of a mixed or medium type	farsighted, self-controlled, accustomed to save, desirous to provide for heirs
Income small, increasing, precarious	20%	10%	5%
Income of a mixed or medium type	10%	5%	2%
Income large, decreasing, assured	5%	2%	1%

If a population is distributed in two dimensions somewhat over the area indicated by this table, with increasing frequencies towards the middle in both directions, and if (as Fisher assumes) potential borrowers and lenders can meet in a common money market, the market rate of interest determined by these numerical indications might be perhaps somewhere in the vicinity of 5%. But in an economy with an erratic and imperfect money market, the person in the upper left-hand corner of the table, who really needs money: poor, short-sighted and weak-

[23] Schumpeter (1) 157, 189, 178; on the medieval background, cf. Pirenne 132.
[24] Fisher 96.

willed, finds no such common estimate of the use value of money to protect him. If he happened to live in the Middle Ages, not infrequently, I suspect, he would have to petition the person safely occupying the bottom right-hand square of Fisher's table: rich, far-sighted, self-controlled, the *usurarius* in person. In this confrontation, the bargaining powers are not evenly distributed and the contract will not end up anywhere near the middle of the table. This table assumes distribution of incomes for consumption purposes ("psychic income"), but the conclusion would not be materially or systematically altered if investment loans were considered. Whether it is the shoemaker's widow or the shoemaker without a shop who approaches the usurer, their needs driving them to agree on a usurious loan might be equally real. If anything, the amount of usury actually paid might be higher in the case of the "consumptive-productive" loan of the shoemaker re-equipping his shop, because he might be lucky (or unlucky) to get the loan at all where the widow's petition might be rejected as too risky.

By a nice little paradox, the psychological principle underlying Böhm-Bawerk's arguments was anticipated by Jevons, an Englishman, while the material principle was anticipated in the Austrian tradition itself by Menger. One might have expected the reverse. The paradox is only apparent. I have no doubt that Aristotle as quoted in *De anima* exerted his influence on British scholars in the tradition to which Bentham and Jevons both belong. But this was the new, rediscovered Greek Aristotle. In no modern school of economists is the survival of the Latin scholastic Aristotle more apparent than in the Austrians, and therefore I am no less sure that it is this influence which speaks in Böhm-Bawerk's "Notlage". In the case of the psychological factors we had to deduce a relationship to the scholastics. In the case of the material factors compelling the acceptance of a usurious loan it speaks loudly in the scholastic texts themselves. To the scholastics a thing was worth what it could be sold for in the absence of ignorance, fraud and *duress*. The principle of economic coercion was applied by them to all kinds of contracts but nowhere more systematically and relentlessly than to money-lending. In fact, in the case of money-lending the principle does not seem to have permitted of any exception. While consent to some commodity prices might be voluntary both in the absolute and in the conditional sense, no one, according to the scholastics, could be said to consent absolutely to a usurious loan. Whenever such acceptance was obtained, it was obtained only conditionally, by force of circumstances. Assuming the absence of fraud and ignorance and deducting for legitimate extrinsic titles, a positive rate of interest on a money loan *must always, because of the sterility of money*, be the result of undue pressure on the borrower.

The idea that the usurer exploits the needs of his neighbour reached the scholastic economists through a long classical and patristic tradition. It is implied, for example, by St Basil[25] and stated with exceptional directness by Lactantius.[26] The further proposition that the borrower under such circumstances pays technically against his true will, owes its deepest basis of authority to St Ambrose as quoted in the *Decretum*, who states that he who accepts usury is guilty of robbery (*rapina*).[27] The *Institutes* of Justinian defines *rapina* as taking goods by force against the owner's will.[28] Peter Lombard did much to popularize this notion in his paragraph on theft in the *Sentences*. "Here", he states, "usury is also prohibited, which comes under robbery".[29] Similarly, Raymond of Peñafort in his classical *Summa* for confessors: "Usury differs little or nothing from robbery".[30]

When William of Auxerre discusses usury in his *Summa aurea* in the early thirteenth century, he cites both the general admonition to support one's neighbour in need and the more specific classification of usury under robbery, then goes on to pose and reply to a question which was to echo throughout the

[25] *Homilia II in Psalmum XIV*, §5; PG 29, 278.
[26] *Divinae institutiones*,VI,18; PL 6, 698-9.
[27] *De bono mortis*; PL 14, 556; cf. *Decretum*,II,14,4,10, ed. Friedberg, 738.
[28] IV,2, introd., cf. IV,1,6.
[29] *Sent.*III.37,4; ed. Quaracchi 1916, II, 719.
[30] P.227.

scholastic tradition. To accept usury is not really to take another's good against the owner's will, says William in opposition to his own teaching, since the borrower is glad to find somebody who charges only lenient usury; therefore, usury is not theft nor any kind of sin. This objection is not valid, according to the author, because it confuses two kinds of voluntariness, namely absolute and comparative voluntariness. In the first sense the borrower does not pay usury willingly; he pays it only because the usurer will not otherwise lend.[31]

If this was written without knowledge of Aristotle's *Ethics*, it seems strangely prescient, since it exactly anticipates the distinction between absolute and conditional consent which the scholastics later found a basis for in Book III of the *Ethics*.[32] Before the rediscovery of Aristotle, the same objection would occasionally be answered conceding the willingness of the borrower but asserting the unwillingness of God! With Aristotle at hand, conditional consent, i.e. *mixed voluntariness* on the part of the borrower, was all that had to be conceded. In the choice between paying usury and going without money, the borrower may choose the first alternative out of need, but except for that condition (which in fact makes the contract ethically illicit) he would not willingly have paid usury; he would rather have had money for free, as he ought to have had. He pays, says Henry of Ghent, *as though forced; because of the need for ready money*.[33] William of Auxerre's argument reappears in Alexander of Hales, in Albert the Great, repeatedly in Aquinas, in Bonaventura, and in Astesanus.[34] Gerardo of Siena opens his

[31] *Summa*,III,21, f.223rb-va.

[32] See above, p.40. The pages where Aristotle discusses the voluntary are in fact among the fragments of an older translation of the *Ethics* than that of Grosseteste, which have been discovered in some scattered manuscripts. However, present evidence does not seem to indicate that this *translatio antiquissima* could have been available to William of Auxerre in the early 1220's when the *Summa aurea* was written.

[33] *Quodl.*II,15, f.40v.

[34] Alexander, pp.914-5; Albert, *Sent.*III,37,13, p.707; Aquinas, *Sent.*III,37,1,6, p.430; *De malo*,XIII,4, p.373, 375; *Sum.theol.*,II-II,78,1, pp.279-280; Bonaventura, *Sent.*III,37, p.835; Astesanus, f.131ra.

long question about usury by stating this objection and in a sense devotes his entire discussion to answering it.

Albert the Great had asked whether the borrower's consent to paying usury does not cause the ownership of the money exceeding the principal to pass to the usurer, a tricky question in connection with restitution. Alexander Lombard picked up Albert's clue and, followed by numerous later authors, applied the distinction between absolute and conditional consent to this question.[35] Olivi, copied by Odonis, concluded his list of arguments against the prohibition of usury by objecting that if usury is sinful on the part of the lender, so it must be on the part of the borrower, because their agreement issues from the consent of both. Olivi counters this by releasing the latter from blame as long as he only consents *necessitate compulsus.*[36] Note, however, that this is not offered as a blanco excuse on the part of the borrower for entering into such contracts.

Odonis found several occasions for discussing usury in his commentary on the *Ethics* of Aristotle. In a question in Book IV, where usury is fleetingly referred to in connection with the virtue of liberality,[37] Odonis asks whether all usury is evil in itself. His first argument in opposition to this is that a usurious contract may be voluntary and profitable on the part of both lender and borrower. Not so, says the commentator. The contract is not voluntary on the part of the borrower, for *necessity forces him to borrow.* Nor is it profitable, for he must repay more than he got.[38] In connection with his analysis of justice in Book V of the *Ethics*, Aristotle raises the famous question as to whether anybody can suffer injustice voluntarily, which he tends to answer in the negative.[39] Odonis states this question

[35] Albert, loc.cit., art.14, pp.709-710; cf. Alexander Lombard, pp.139-141, 186-7; Pisanus, f.186ra; Hassia, f.201rb; Angelus, f.365va; Trovamala, f.259rb; Ariosto, f.d_3 ra; Biel, *Sent.*IV,15,11, f.QQ_2 rb.

[36] Olivi, f.300vb, ff.303vb-304ra; Odonis, f.90v; 93r; cf. also Durandus of Saint-Pourçain, *Sent.*III,37,4, ff.281vb- 282ra.

[37] See above, p.55.

[38] Q.IV,20; ed. Bresica 1482, ff.P_3vb-P_4ra.

[39] 1138a.

formally and poses some exceptions from the general rule, such as when voluntariness is only conditional as it is for example where usury is paid on money.[40] The early commentaries in question form on the *Politics* of Aristotle also employ the principle of conditional consent when discussing usury in Book I.[41] Buridan followed all these three leads in his questions on the two works.[42] Through these various channels the proposition that usury is extracted by force of circumstances reached the late scholastics like Bernardino of Siena, Antonino of Florence, and Francis of Platea.[43] The borrower only pays usury because the lender will not otherwise lend, says the latter. Therefore the lender can truly be said to take the borrower's money against his will – in the absolute sense that is, if not in the conditional sense.

I have produced these lists of names and recorded the traditions in such detail in order to commit myself fully to the testable thesis that the principle described was universally accepted and driven through with complete consistency. Its crucial point is that it invalidates usury unconditionally. It condemns, not just usury above a certain permissible maximum rate or usury obtained with more than a certain degree of duress, but all usury at any rate whatsoever. While in commodity exchange the parties were free to bargain about terms and the moralists were prepared to accept varying terms as fair outcome, bargaining which issued in any positive rate of usury was out of the question. If usury was paid at all, free will in the absolute sense was *ipso facto* violated. The doctrine of the just price in commodity exchange and the doctrine of usury proceed analogously in so far as they both apply the principles of cost and indemnity and the principle of the irrelevancy of the utility of the opposite party. But the analogy breaks down with the checks and correctives provided by a common estimate.[44]

40 Q.V,18; ed.cit., f.Y_8va.

41 Paris BN lat.16089, Q.I.28, f.282va; cf. Bologna BU 1625, Q.I.26, f.63ra.

42 *Comm.Eth.*, Q.IV,6, f.76ra-b and Q.V,23, f.111ra; *Comm.Pol.*, Q.I,12, f.18rb.

43 Bernardino, Sermo 36,3,12, pp.219-220; Sermo 38,1,8, p.251; Antonino, *Summa*,II,ii,7,1-2, coll.399-401; Platea, f.84v.

44 See above, p.36.

In the case of money, no resort can be had to a rough guess as to what the market rate might be, allowing for limits of tolerance, as in the case of commodity exchange. Usury permitted of no tolerance at all. The rate must be identically zero. It is not as though the scholastics could deduce a zero market rate hypothetically on the basis of theoretical insight into the kind of stationary economy they envisaged, thus anticipating a modern inference. But they stated it nevertheless, in the Aristotelian terms of duress and sterility. Not all of them employed both the sterility argument and the argument from duress, though a comparison of my lists of references will show that many did so. Explicitly or implicitly made, the inference is patent: *Usury is robbery because money is barren.* No one will willingly pay more for a thing than it is worth, and the use of money is worth nothing, for money cannot breed. The modern inference is close enough as well: if duress could be ruled out, as in a free, competitive money market, then the market rate of the use of money would tend to zero.

*

To say that this system rests on foundations in Aristotle's philosophy is not to explain fully why the scholastics built it and defended it for so long. What ethical purpose did it serve? That question is too broad; let me just, by way of conclusion, make two personal suggestions, one general, the other relating to the sterility doctrine. I believe quite generally that if we seek to locate the purpose of scholastic economic ethics in the macro-economy, then we are on the wrong track. To think of guiding the total economy in desired directions requires an instrumental conception of economic variables which was as yet foreign to most of these authors. Thus, for example, if it is correct (as has been alleged) that the prohibition of usury favoured agriculture and if some scholastic author may have remarked upon this, the fact and the remark are both, in all likelihood, purely accidental to the doctrine. The ends envisaged by our authors related to man *qua* generalized individual, not to man *en masse*. Their theory of usury was in a sense an exploitation theory, but they knew nothing of aggregate factors of production, one exploiting the other. Exploitation to them was exploitation of individual man by individual man. Theirs was still a personalistic ethic; it was inherited from Scripture and the Fathers and partly confirmed by Roman law. Prohibition of usury protected the needy borrower – including the needy agriculturist, but the argument did not aspire to aggregation. It also protected his wealthy neighbour from the sin of enrichment.

The "spirit of capitalism" with which Aristotle was countered in the sixteenth century was also "justified" on the individual level. It is one of the merits of the Weber thesis to have focused on this fact. Social justification came later and transformed the ideology. The spirit which found its most publicized popular voice in Calvin is one which acknowledges our duty towards the needy but sees no sin in enrichment either. It is in this that it is most fundamentally un-Aristotelian. As such it also denies that money is sterile. What a frivolous idea, says Calvin; money is as fruitful as anything else. Of course, taking usury from the poor is wrong. But if someone lends money to a neighbour richer than himself, why should he be denied a share in its fruits?[45] It is a valid enough remark. The scholastics saw no feasible way to discriminate between degrees and qualities of need. So they legislated with a view to the most pressing (and perhaps, after all, the most typical) cases, where the borrower is truly unfree and in need of protection. In consequence, some resourceful medieval entrepreneurs may have pocketed some unreasonable profits while some reasonable loans may have been rejected in fear of the sin of usury.

The snag is that discrimination according to "true" need is impossible on the basis of *justice*. If money bears fruit, if it has a possible use value, then to forgo this value is not justice but *charity*. Calvin says so himself: To lend for free is the true test of charity (*caritatis probatio*).[46] Justice and charity are twin sisters,

[45] *De usuris*, CR 38, 247; *In Ezechiel*,18, CR 68, 431-2.
[46] *In Deut.*,23, CR 52, 680.

said Thomas Hobbes. But charity is the weaker sister. It is difficult in one's daily dealings to forgo fruits that are *rightly* one's own. The positive argument made by Turgot against the scholastics (before countering their doctrine in three points) is that ownership of money brings with it a *right* to lend at interest. By what strange caprice of morals or legislation should this be prohibited?[47] On the ethical premises of Turgot and his contemporaries, prohibition of usury was indeed unreasonable. But the annals of capitalism (from way back in the writings of Calvin, or Turgot, or wherever they started) show that charity alone provides scant protection for those in need of credit. What the sterility doctrine enabled the scholastics to insist on is that he who takes usury is not only uncharitable but unjust.

Looking back on a system like this, through a distance of time which has changed our economies, our economics and our ethics, it is easy to brush it off as irrelevant. It "never made sense at all", says one of the augurs of modern growth theory.[48] It is tempting to overreact to dismissals like that by making more sense than there actually was, through deductions which might have surprised the scholastics themselves. Undoubtedly there were loose ends hanging about in their system and sometimes those loose ends were snapped bowstrings. How could it be otherwise? It is only when we ourselves possess a consistent theory of interest that we can blame another age for the lack of it. Nevertheless, the sterility of money may not have been such a sterile concept. I would caution against defending it for the reasons voiced by some other leading modern economists, who have directed much more favourable comments at scholastic economics. Wicksell is one of these; Keynes is another.[49] What they saw in the sterility doctrine was an honest and theoretically meritorious attempt to separate returns on money from returns on real capital. But these authors were also focusing on economies in growth. In the context of such an economy, the

[47] Op.cit., p.122; cf. above, note 2 to Chapter 4.
[48] Harrod 158.
[49] Wicksell II, 190-1, Keynes 351-2.

sterility of money is an empty proposition, just as the physical concept of money has become nearly empty. As I would rather prefer to state it by way of conclusion, the proposition intuitively grasped by the medieval scholastics, and perhaps containing an element of truth for which they claimed the support of Aristotle's *Politics*, is that money in the sense of coin is sterile and can breed no surplus when it serves merely to facilitate exchange in economies which breed no surplus.

Bibliography

Bardenhewer, Otto: *Geschichte der altkirchlichen Literatur.* I-V. Freiburg im Br. 1913-32.

Barker, Ernest: *The Political Thought of Plato and Aristotle.* London 1906.

Bettoni, Efrem: *Le dottrine filosofiche di Pier di Giovanni Olivi.* Milan 1959.

Böhm-Bawerk, Eugen von: *Kapital und Kapitalzins.* 2. Aufl. I-II. Innsbruck 1900-1902.

Brants, Victor: *L'Economie politique au moyen Age.* Louvain 1895.

Cannan, E., W.D.Ross, J.Bonar and P.H.Wicksteed: "Who said 'Barren Metal'?". *Economica* 2 (1922) 105-111.

Cuyás, Manuel: "El tratado 'De praescriptione', obra de Gerardo de Siena († 1336), existe aún manoscrito e impreso". *Gregorianum* 41 (1960) 701-8.

Cossa, Luigi: *An Introduction to the Study of Political Economy.* London 1893.

Defourny, Maurice: *Aristote. Etude sur la 'Politique'.* Paris 1932.

De Roover, Raymond: *San Bernardino of Siena and Sant'Antonino of Florence. The Two Great Economic Thinkers of the Middle Ages.* Boston 1967.

Endemann, Wilhelm: *Studien in der romanisch-kanonistischen Wirtschafts- und Rechtslehre.* I-II. Berlin 1874-83.

Fanfani, Amintore: *Le origini dello spirito capitalistico in Italia.* Milan 1933.

Fetter, Frank: *Economic Principles.* New York 1915.

Fisher, Irving: *The Theory of Interest.* New York 1930.

Funk, Franz X. (1): *Zins und Wucher.* Tübingen 1868.

– (2): "Ueber die ökonomischen Anschauungen der mittelalterlichen Theologen". *Zeitschrift für die gesamte Staatswissenschaft* 25 (1869) 125-175.

– (3): *Geschichte des kirchlichen Zinsverbotes.* Tübingen 1876.

Gordon, Barry: *Economic Analysis before Adam Smith.* London 1975.

Hamelin, A.-M.: *Un traité de morale économique au XIVe siècle. Le Tractatus de usuris de maître Alexandre d'Alexandrie. Analecta mediaevalia Namurcensia* 14 (1962).

Harrod, R.F.: *Towards a Dynamic Economics.* London 1948.

Hauser, Henri: *Les débuts du capitalisme.* Paris 1927.

Jevons, W.Stanley: *The Theory of Political Economy.* London 1871.

Keynes, John Maynard: *The General Theory of Employment, Interest, and Money.* London 1936.

Langholm, Odd (1): *Price and Value in the Aristotelian Tradition.* Bergen 1979.

– (2): "Economic freedom in scholastic thought". *History of Political Economy* 14 (1982) 260-283.

– (3): *Wealth and Money in the Aristotelian Tradition.* Bergen 1983.

Marshall, Alfred: *Principles of Economics.* Ed.5. London 1907.

Menger, Carl: *Grundsätze der Volkswirtschaftslehre.* Vienna 1871.
Newman, W.L.: *The Politics of Aristotle.* I-IV. Oxford 1887-1902.
Noonan, John T., jr.: *The Scholastic Analysis of Usury.* Cambridge, Mass. 1957.
O'Brien, George: *An Essay on Mediaeval Economic Teaching.* London 1920.
Pacetti, D.: "Un trattato sulle usure e le restituzioni di Pietro di Giovanni Olivi, falsamente attribuito a Fr. Gerardo da Siena". *Archivum Franciscanum Historicum* 46 (1953) 448-457.
Pirenne, Henri: *Economic and Social History of Medieval Europe.* London 1936.
Rambaud, Joseph: *Histoire des doctrines économiques.* Paris 1899.
Samuelson, Paul A.: "Dynamics, statics, and the stationary state". *The Review of Economic Statistics* 25 (1943) 58-68.
Schaub, Franz: *Der Kampf gegen den Zinswucher, ungerechten Preis und unlautern Handel im Mittelalter.* Freiburg im Br. 1905.
Schumpeter, Joseph A. (1): *The Theory of Economic Development.* Cambridge, Mass. 1934.
– (2): *History of Economic Analysis.* London 1954.
Sombart, Werner: *Der Bourgeois.* Munich 1913.
Spicciani, Amleto: *La mercatura e la formazione del prezzo nella riflessione teologica medioevale.* Rome 1977.
Troeltsch, Ernst: *Die Soziallehren der christlichen Kirchen und Gruppen. Gesammelte Schriften,* Vol.I. Tübingen 1922.
Weber, Max: *The Protestant Ethic and the Spirit of Capitalism.* London 1930.
Wicksell, Knut: *Lectures on Political Economy.* I-II. London 1934-5.